Tonkinese Cats

The Tonkinese Cat Owner's Manual

Tonkinese Cat care, personality, grooming, health, training, costs and feeding all included.

By

Elliott Lang

Author: Elliott Lang

Published by: IMB Publishing

Table of Contents

Table of Contents

Table of Contents

Table of Contents

Table of Contents

Table of Contents

Acknowledgements

I wish to convey special thanks to my family members who gave me the time and space I needed to write this book.

I would also like to pay special thanks to my friends and colleagues whose input proved valuable in obtaining all the necessary information I needed to develop this book.

Special thanks to the following organizations/associations for their valuable support;

The International Cat Association (TICA)
The American Cat Fanciers Association (CFA)
The Governing Council of the Cat Fancy (UK)
America Pet Products Association
Cat Owners Association of Western Australia
American Animal Hospital Association (AAHA)
Worldwide Pet Owners Association
The South African Cat Council
The Winn Feline Association
Feline Council of South Australia
The Governing Council of the Cat Fancy of South Australia (GCCFSA)
Cat Fanciers' Federation (CFF)
Canadian Cat Association
Tonkinese Breed Association (USA)
Tonkinese Breed Club (UK)
Tonkinese Cat Club (UK)
Tonkinese Breed Council (USA)
Tonks West (USA)

Chapter 1 – Introduction

Cats have always fascinated me. Having lived with them, other pets and farm animals for a long time, this valuable opportunity has given me a lot of experience in dealing with and handling both pets and farm animals.

My parents used to live in a remote rural area where they kept pets and reared livestock since I was born. The cats were particularly of great interest to me and still are. This interest set me up for a long journey of interacting with cat breeders from across the world, breeders from whom I have learnt a lot relating to different cat breeds.

Of all cat breeds, the Tonkinese breed captured my attention to a point where the cat is now one of my favorite cats. I indeed have two of them as pets and can authoritatively claim to be in a good position to introduce it to cat lovers and others interested in having the cat as a pet.

With a very interesting history, this breed of cat has come a long way and is one of the best cat breeds to have at home as a pet, at least from my personal experience.

This is probably the most loving, attention-seeking and entertaining cat you can have at home as a pet. It is not surprising that the breed is a favorite of many homeowners and cat lovers. It is indeed because of their popularity that the breed is to be found in most breeder catteries. Furthermore, the Tonkinese breed is one breed of cat with many clubs established by Tonkinese cat owners across the world.

Tonkinese kitten and cat prices varies and depends on several factors. Some of the factors include breeder location and whether or not a kitten or cat's family tree is a "show" or "pet" line. In general, breeder prices for pedigree Tonkinese kitten pets ranges between $350 and $500 (£210 and £300). Breeder price for an adult Tonkinese pet cat ranges between $400 and $700 (£240 and £415).

Prices for purebred Tonkinese kittens and cats for show tend to be on the higher side because of amount of work that goes into breeding and training them. While Tonkinese show kittens range between $500 and $1000 (£300 and £595), show cats go for between $700 and $1,500 (£415 and £890).

You can also opt to buy a Tonkinese kitten or cat from a cat rescue center or shelter, where the price for kittens ranges between $250 and $400 (£148 and £210) while that of cats is between $350 and $450 (£210 and £265). It is important to point out that these are average prices. You may find the price of Tonkinese kittens and cats either higher or lower, depending on your location and other factors.

Chapter 2 – The Tonkinese Cat

History/Origin

The Tonkinese cat is really not a new breed of cat. Indeed, Tonkinese-like cats are known to have existed as early as the 19th century. A good example is a female cat named Wong Mau, a hybrid Burmese cat that was imported into the USA (California) in 1930 by the founder of the American Burmese type of cat, Dr. Joseph Thomson.

The modern Tonkinese cat is however the result of crossbreeding between Siamese and Burmese breeds of cats. Through a Canadian breeding program, the intention was to develop a unique breed of cat that, although borrows from both the Siamese and the Burmese, remained distinct on its own, with a unique appearance and lively personality. The Tonkinese was therefore developed from hybrid cats.

The need to develop the Tonkinese breed was by design rather than by chance. Both Siamese and Burmese cat breeders then generally considered the two poor quality cat breeds. It is because of that consideration that Milan Greer, a feline expert living in New York who had hitherto had Siamese and Burmese cats, resolved to crossbreed the two in the 1950s. The litter he obtained was encouraging; a cat with an appearance that was between that of a Siamese and a Burmese with dark spots and a rich mahogany body.

Encouraged by the result, Greer continued with his breeding program, which in real sense was an experiment. His breeding program yielded chocolate-brown cats with dark brown spots. Although the litters he obtained became very popular, he abandoned his breeding program in 1960s after naming the unique breed of cat the Golden Siamese. Even so, Greer's efforts did not go to waste. One Edith Lux picked up from where Greer had left off, changing the name of the breed from Golden Siamese to Tonkinese. Lux literally borrowed the name from the Gulf of Tonkin in Thailand from where both Siamese and Burmese cats originated.

Although both Greer and Lux made great efforts in developing the Tonkinese cat breed, credit goes to Margaret Conroy, a Canadian cat breeder who picked up the Siamese/Burmese breeding program and registered the new breed with the Canadian Cat Association. While Ms Conroy was busy in Canada breeding the Tonkinese and promoting it, Jane Barletta of New Jersey, herself a cat breeder, was also busy breeding the same and promoting the new breed. The efforts by the two ladies paid off when a number of cat breeders both in Canada and US got interested in joining in. Jane Barletta in particular did a lot of work of breeding the Tonkinese cat and promoting it through newspaper advertisements and TV shows.

It is because of Baretta's efforts that the Tonkinese Breed Club was established in the USA with membership largely made up of cat breeders. The club set out to identify and establish the breed standard and approached the CFA Board for registration, a request that was initially denied. This prompted the club to restrict itself to cat shows. The breed was eventually registered by CFA in 1978, paving the way for establishment of The Tonkinese Breed Association in 1979, an association that remains an affiliate of CFA to date.

Although the Tonkinese became registered by CFA as a distinct cat breed, the breed did not receive championship status. This only came years later in 1984. By then, the breed had been shown in over 200 CFA-organized cat shows. Breeding of Tonkinese from Siamese and Burmese cats effectively ended with breeders focusing on breeding Tonkinese for Tonkinese cats to preserve established standards.

Although an intermediate breed of cat, the Tonkinese does not in any way represent either the Siamese or the Burmese. Indeed, the Tonkinese cannot be mistaken for either of the two. Although recognized in the USA and North America including Canada as a distinct cat breed, the breed is not recognized by some cat registries and clubs across the world. For instance, the breed only gained recognition by Britain's Governing Council of the Cat Fancy (GCCF) in 1991. Its growing popularity with cat lovers, owners and breeders is however not in doubt. The breed is indeed ranked 7th as the most popular breed of cat in the USA.

Myths Associated with Tonkinese cats
Like with all cat breeds, the Tonkinese breed too has its share of myths that are otherwise not true. Some of the myths associated with the Tonkinese breed extend to both the Burmese and Siamese breed of cats.

One of the most common myths associated with the Tonkinese cat was exclusive to Thai King and that the cat only left Thailand when it was smuggled out. There is no doubt that Tonkinese-looking cats had lived in other parts of the world. Furthermore, the Tonkinese's early breeding program is well documented and the breed is indeed referred to as one of the human-engineered breed of cats.

The other myth associated with Tonkinese cats relates to worship. Many have come to believe, wrongly, that the Tonkinese, together with both the Burmese and Siamese were worshiped by Thai people, who dedicated special temples for them. This is purely a myth since there is nowhere in history indicating that Thai people ever worshiped cats. What is true is that Budhism, which is practiced in Thailand, advocates for compassion and kindness towards animals and Thai monks used to take care of cats by feeding them.

Pros and Cons of Owning a Tonkinese Cat

Pros

It is very important that you carefully consider whether or not the Tonkinese cat is the right cat for you to have in the house as a pet. From the onset, this breed of cat is one of the most affectionate cats you can find. A Tonk shows appreciation and makes your house very lively.

This is also the best cat you can have for company. You never get bored when you have a Tonk as a pet. In addition to showing off its skills, the cat is very talkative and will entertain you for hours on end.

The Tonkinese is one of the low-maintenance cats you can find. Not only is the breed less susceptible to hereditary feline diseases/health conditions, it is also a very health breed that does not become sick easily, unless you expose it to illnesses.

Cons

The Tonkinese is a very active cat. It loves heights and is very fond of jumping all over, which increases risk of injury.

The Tonkinese cat can be very talkative, which you may not find to be comfortable, especially when you need some peace of mind.

The Tonkinese can be very destructive when bored. Apart from jumping all over, the cat has the tendency of playing with precious items and disorganizing everything that you arrange. You can however manage this through proper training.

Chapter 3 – Appearance of the Tonkinese Cat

Commonly referred to as the Tonk, the Tonkinese is of medium size and muscular just like its ancestor, the Burmese. It is however heavier than it appears to be. Everything about the cat is pointed; the ears, darker feet and legs, facial marks. The head is gently rounded but wedge-shaped. This is one of the most active, attention-seeking and acting cats you can have at home as a pet.

Head

The Tonkinese features a head that is slightly wedged with a blunted muzzle. The ears are characteristically set outside of the head. The ears remain medium-sized and appear rounded. Of all the cat's features, it is the eyes that make it stand out. The cat has almond-shaped and sparkling aqua eye colour, which can be green, golden or blue depending on coat pattern. The cat's eye colour no doubt lies between the Siamese eye's sapphire blue and the Burmese eye's deep gold.

Body

The Tonkinese cat's body is neither short nor long. It is actually a slim cat that is otherwise elegant and muscular. Although it appears light, it is heavy when carried.

Coat

This is a cat with a wonderful coat. While the coat remains darker at the base, which is a Siamese's coat colour, the hair is characteristically thick, silky and shiny, with dark spots. The hair is short and lies close to the body, which negates the need for regular grooming.

Colour

You can find the Tonkinese cat in varied colours. However, CFA only recognizes four colours; medium brown, champagne, blue and platinum. You are also likely to find a Tonkinese cat in twelve other colours including red. A major point of note is that regardless of colour, a Tonkinese will have a clear coat pattern referred to as mink (US) or solid (UK).

Body Weight

Tonkinese cats are heavier that what they portray in appearance. While a male cat weighs on average between 4 and 5 kg (8 and 12 pounds), a female weighs between 3 and 4 kg (6 and 8 pounds).

Temperament/Personality

Like its Siamese and Burmese ancestors, the Tonkinese is outgoing, friendly, confident, intelligent, moderately active, playful and at times very vocal. It is a cat that always wants to make its presence felt. In addition to socializing easily with both adults and children, the Tonkinese is very welcoming to other pets including dogs.

This is one breed always out to know what goes around. Its voice is similar to that of a Burmese; soft, sweet but persistent. This breed of cat is often considered to be dog-like because of its jumping and fetching behaviour. The cat particularly likes and enjoys jumping to high places.

Chapter 4 – Psychology of the Tonkinese Cat

Aggression

The Tonkinese is never known to be aggressive. It is a gentle cat that is only active, playful and very affectionate. The cat is never aggressive under normal circumstances. It really enjoys human company and that of other pets.

This does not mean in any way that the cat cannot develop aggressive tendencies. However, unlike other breeds of cats that acquire aggressive tendencies genetically, the Tonkinese can only develop aggressive tendencies when subjected to harsh treatment and lack of proper care. A cat brought up in a harsh environment where it is subjected to constant mistreatment will naturally develop aggressive tendencies as a way of defending itself.

Cats are, by nature, territorial beings. A Tonkinese cat will naturally mark the house as its territory but unlike other breeds of cats, the cat will readily welcome any other cat or pet for companionship.

Intelligence

Intelligence here refers to your Tonkinese cat's capacity to learn, solve problems and adapt to its surroundings. From the onset, Tonkinese cats adapt to new environments very easily so long as they are well treated and provided for. Kittens in particular get used to new environments very fast because they set out to explore any new environment they are introduced to.

The Tonkinese cat is one of the most intelligent cats. The cat easily gets accustomed to routines at home and will do everything to please its master by sticking to a set routine. It is also because of their high intelligence that the cat resorts to destructive activities purely for amusement. This particularly happens when the cat is not involved in play activities to a point where it feels bored.

The cat has very high memory, which contributes to its level of intelligence. The play activities the cat engages in do not only serve as its way of life or behavior; it learns a lot from such activities and it is only appropriate that you have many but different cat toys. Play activities help them in exercising their minds and in honing their natural skills.

Curiosity

A Tonkinese cat's high level of intelligence coupled with its playfulness makes it very curious, especially in new surroundings. Although the cat thrives well both indoors and outdoors, it is better to keep it as an indoor pet. It will however venture outdoors occasionally to explore the exterior surroundings.

Rubbing

Although not adopted from the wild, the Tonkinese cat has the natural instinct that all cats have of marking its territory within the house and everything therein. This is very common with a male cat that rubs itself on furniture, walls and on your legs. This is natural behavior that should not be of serious concern. While rubbing itself against everything in sight, your Tonkinese cat releases pheromones through its scent glands located on its tail and other parts of the body. You have the option of neutering/spaying the cat in case this behaviour is on the extreme side.

Body Language

Of all signs and signals, the signs and signals that cats send out through their body language are very important. Your Tonkinese cat's body posture at any given time serves as an indication of its state of mind. The cat will behave in a particular manner when it is in a relaxed position. Whether simply lying down or sitting, it will most likely have its legs bent, the tail loosely wrapped around its shoulders or head. These will be accompanied by normal breathing.

There are times when your cat will exhibit alert body posture, in which case it will lie down on its belly with its back horizontal. Although its breathing may be normal, it will have its legs either bent or extended with the tail curved towards the back. It may twitch its tail from one side to another. This is usually the behavior of a cat focused on something such as a live prey.

Tensed cats usually present body posture in such a way that the back remains lower than their upper body while lying down. Your Tonkinese cat may be moving forwards or backwards with its hind legs bent and the front legs extended. The tail may be curled downwards or curled up. This is usually a clear sign of aggression.

Your Tonkinese cat and a female one in particular will once in a while present a body posture where the back of its body is the only part of the body that remains visible with the front part less visible. This can happen when it is lying down on its belly or when in a standing position. The breathing in most cases is usually fast with the tail very close to the body in a curled position. This is usually a sign of anxiety. It can also be a sign that your cat is on heat in case it is not spayed.

You should find it easy to know when your cat is either terrified or fearful. It will most likely be in a crouched position on its paws with its entire body shaking. The tail will remain close to its body. Although medium in size, it will try to increase its size further as a way of fending off the threat.

Your Tonkinese cat will not only serve you as a pet and a companion; it will also serve to warn you of possible dangers within the house or compound. Any body language sign or signal your cat sends out needs immediate attention since it may notice a threat long before you do.

Vocals

A Tonkinese cat that is well provided for and accorded the necessary attention can be very vocal. The cat is known to chatter, particularly when it is contended and happy. There are also times when the cat seems to "talk" in sentences and paragraphs. This is especially when in need of food or attention. It is always recommended that you listen to your Tonk as it "speaks" since failure to do so may force it to look for an alternative way of expressing itself, which can be very destructive.

Panting

Although cats generally do not pant like dogs, there are times when your Tonk will pant. This will most likely be when travelling in a car, when stressed, when anxious and when on heat among other situations. You must however take note of excessive panting, as the same may be a sign of illness.

House Soiling

House soiling is the most disturbing behaviour you will most likely observe your cat engage in. House soiling simply means urinating or defecating all over instead of using a provided litter box.

While it is perfectly normal for your cat to urinate (spray) outside its litter box, defecating outside the litter box can be because of other reasons. Your Tonk will most likely spray outside its litter box as one way of marking its territory. Unlike regular urination, your cat will spray while standing and probably with one leg raised instead of squatting. Spraying becomes common when you have several cats in the house, in which case the dominant cat (usually a male) marks its territory.

Urination and defecation outside the litter box can be because of several reasons, one of which is a medical problem. Any inflammation of your cat's urinary tract will cause frequent and sometimes painful urination. Because it is most likely to associate the pain it experiences with the litter box, it will avoid the it. The other reason may be because of the urgency to urinate when the litter box is in a different room.

Another reason for house soiling can simply be aversion. Your Tonk may find the litter box unsuitable for several reasons including bad odour, high-sided litter box, dirty litter box, distasteful litter box and inappropriate location of the litter box. You must therefore always keep the litter box clean and tidy.

House soiling can be very traumatizing. It is therefore very important that you take all the necessary measures to find out why your cat engages in this form of behaviour. It is always recommended that you take your cat to a vet for assessment in case there is no apparent reason for regular house soiling.

Poor Social Behaviour

Cats in general are never born to exhibit irrational behaviour. A cat's behaviour is never based on its emotions unless it is exposed to extreme mistreatment and poor living conditions. Any cat that exhibits unbecoming behaviour normally does so as a way of hitting back at the owner for mistreatment. Cats do also resort to behaving in an unusual manner due to high stress levels and anxiety.

Although generally very friendly, affectionate and playful, the Tonkinese cat is very fond of engaging in extroverted behaviour. You do not need to take this to mean unbecoming behaviour because this breed of cat displays a high level of intelligence, energy and curiosity. This is a cat that likes to show off and does everything it can to attract your attention. A Tonk that engages in extreme extroverted behaviour is usually one that is left alone most of the time without human company or that of another cat or pet. A properly trained Tonk will not only be friendly and well behaved but also welcoming to family members and strangers alike.

Chapter 5 – Buying a Tonkinese Kitten or Cat

Although the Tonkinese breed of cat has been around for some time, it has not become to be as popular as other cat breeds that have been around for the same time. This can partly be attributed to the fact that the breed is not yet recognized by some cat registries as a distinct breed of cat. Even so, the breed's popularity is fast rising as many cat lovers and owners realize that it is one of the best cats to have at home as a pet.

There are several ways through which you can gain possession of a Tonkinese cat:

From a Neighbour or Friend
This is the easiest way to acquire a Tonkinese kitten or cat. You can have a neighbour with kittens, in which case you may buy or simply receive one or several for free as a gift. This way of acquiring cats or any other pet for that matter is however not recommended for several reasons. Firstly, the kitten you buy may not necessarily be pure-breed. Secondly, you may acquire kittens with serious health problems.

From a Cat Rescue Center

You are most likely to find a general cat rescue center offering different breeds of cats for sale. It can however be very difficult to find a Tonkinese cat at a rescue center. This is because they are not all that popular with homeowners and those who have them go to great lengths to make their cats comfortable so as not to lose them. Even so, gaining possession of a Tonk from a rescue center if you are lucky to find one is not recommended because caretakers are not necessarily knowledgeable about them. This simply means that you will not receive the necessary advice on how to maintain your cat in the most recommended way. Should you be lucky to find a Tonk at a rescue center, it is highly recommended that you take the cat to a veterinarian as soon as possible for health check-ups.

From a Pet Store

There are dedicated pet stores that specialize in selling Tonkinese kittens and cats. While some of such stores are breeder outlets, others are those that are operated by individual owners who may not have sufficient information regarding the breed. You may therefore consider buying a kitten or cat from a breeder.

From a Breeder

There are breeders across the world that specialize in breeding Tonkinese cats. Most of these breeders happen to have once been proud owners of the cat and were forced to graduate to breeders owing to the small number of breeders available. Because of the breed's limited popularity, most of the breeders happen to be general breeders, in which case they are also involved in breeding other breed of cat.

Well-established Tonkinese cat breeders around the world are members of different organizations and associations. Such organizations/associations include The International Cat Association (TICA), American Cat Fanciers Association (CFA), The Governing Council of the Cat Fancy (UK), South African Cat

Council, Feline Council of South Australia, Cat Fanciers Federation (CFF), Canadian Cat Association, Cat Owners Association of Western Australia, Tonkinese Cat Association (USA), Tonkinese Breed Club (UK) and Tonkinese Cat Club (UK) among other organizations/associations.

Different Tonkinese cat owners in specific regions and locations around the world have also formed their own clubs for the purpose of sharing information about the cat and promoting the breed.

How to Choose a Breeder

Buying a kitten, cat or any other pet for that matter from either a general breeder or a specialized breeder provides for several benefits. Although buying from a breeder can be expensive depending on your location, the quality of a kitten or cat you buy is no doubt high. This is because breeders put in a lot of effort in ensuring that a kitten or cat you buy is not only purebred but also free of hereditary health problems associated with the Tonkinese breed.

Although buying a Tonkinese kitten or cat from a breeder is highly recommended, it is very important that you choose a breeder carefully. Doing so makes it possible for you to buy a healthy cat.

One of the most important things you need to look into is whether or not a breeder is a member of a national, regional or international cat association. Such breeders do adhere to a code of ethics formulated by associations. A reputable breeder should be available for consultation when it becomes necessary long after purchasing your cat.

It is also very important that you ascertain whether or not a breeder you plan to buy from has all the requisite certifications and in particular, certifications relating to the screening of genetic health problems. Perhaps a good way to choose the right breeder lies in consulting with your local veterinarian, who is in a better position to know reputable local Tonkinese cat breeders.

Questions to Ask

The most important thing to do when visiting a cat breeder with the aim of buying a kitten or cat is to ask questions. A reputable breeder should be willing to help you understand a Tonkinese kitten or cat. Most reputable breeders allow you to see all the Tonkinese cat litters in the cattery before you choose one or several to buy.

Your initial observation about a kitten or cat should from the first instance inform you on a kitten's or cat's appropriateness. In addition to a cattery's overall cleanliness, a kitten or cat you are interested in should look healthy and clean. In particular, a kitten's or cat's hips and backbone need to be well covered. Likewise, a kitten or cat must not exhibit a potbelly, which is in most cases a sign of worm infestation.

A kitten's or cat's eyes should be bright and free of any sign of discharge. You need to examine the ears, which should not have any signs of particles. Presence of black particles in the ears is in most cases a sign of flea infestation.

There are a number of critical questions that you need to ask a breeder before you make any financial commitment. A reputable breeder should not only answer your questions; he/she should be prepared to answer in detail. Asking some or all questions relating to the following will be of great benefit to you.

Experience

You need to choose a breeder with some years of experience in breeding cats and in particular Tonkinese cats. It is also important to ascertain whether or not a breeder participates in cat shows. Breeders who participate in cat shows do not only have the experience but valuable knowledge as well, knowledge that will benefit you, as the breeder will certainly share the it with you.

Breeding Style

It is very important that you ascertain a breeder's breeding style before you buy. A knowledgeable breeder will normally adopt a breeding style that addresses a Tonkinese cat's health problems. Buying from such a breeder ensures that you buy a kitten or cat with very minimal health issues to deal with.

Vaccinations

Like with all other animals, it is good to ascertain if a breeder's Tonkinese kittens or cats receive the requisite vaccinations before they are sold off. It is very important that you only buy a vaccinated kitten or cat to reduce veterinary costs. If you are prepared to pay a bit more, you can cover these costs yourself.

Guarantees

Although not offered by all cat breeders, buying a kitten or cat with a health guarantee can be very beneficial to you. A cat that you buy can fall ill within days of buying and it is only appropriate that you have some level of guarantee.

Certification

In addition to a breeder's certification, it is good to ascertain whether or not the parents of a kitten you are about to buy are certified. This simply means that a kitten whose parents are certified will not be at risk of suffering genetic health conditions.

These are just a few of the many critical questions that you need to ask a breeder. Doing so makes it possible for you to buy a quality kitten or cat that is easy to maintain in terms of veterinary costs. You may however need to realize that finding a specialized Tonkinese cat breeder can be difficult since most turn out to be general cat breeders.

How to Choose a Healthy Tonkinese Kitten/Cat

Whether buying a Tonkinese kitten or cat, identifying a healthy one to buy should not be a problem. In addition to physical observation and examination, the other way to ascertain a kitten's health status is to ask a breeder to see the kitten's parents. Tonkinese cats are generally playful, which should also be evident in their kitten.

Undertaking a pre-purchase examination is also very important. A reputable cat breeder will normally allow you to visit with a qualified veterinarian for such examination. A vet should be in a position to perform a number of routine tests including the cat's general blood work, viral tests, stool/urine analysis and general physical examination.

Purebred or Crossbred and Why

This is one of the most important decisions you have to make when planning to buy a cat. Like with other cat breeds, you will come across purebred and crossbred Tonkinese kittens and cats. However, breeders can restrict themselves to selling purebred Tonkinese kittens and cats.

Buying a purebred Tonkinese kitten or cat can be beneficial to you, considering that you end up with a cat whose personality and characteristics you know perfectly well. Furthermore, buying a purebred cat makes it possible for you to deal with known health challenges that the breed is susceptible to. Although crossbred Tonkinese cats do face similar health challenges as purebred, theirs may be complicated to deal with because of genetic alterations. The cost of purebred Tonkinese kittens and cats is usually higher than that of crossbred.

Where to Buy

Even though the Tonkinese cat's popularity is currently not comparable to that of other breeds of cats, the number of breeders venturing into breeding Tonkinese cats is rising at a steady pace. The rise in the number of Tonkinese cat breeders is a clear indication that many cat lovers no longer believe the myths that have for a long time been associated with the breed. Indeed, many cat lovers are now appreciating the breed's personality.

Finding a reputable Tonkinese cat breeder to buy from should not be a problem. Reputable Tonkinese cat breeders are members of both national and international associations and organizations. Such associations and organizations draw their breeder membership from across the world, making it easy for you to find a breeder located near your location. You have the option of contacting any association or organization for information about available breeders to contact a chosen breeder directly. They include the following:

Tonkinese Breed Association
(www.tonkinesebreedassociation.org)

This association is suited for US residents who wish to purchase quality purebred Tonkinese kittens and cats. It has a large database of Tonkinese cat breeders located in different parts of USA.

Tonkinese Cat Club (www.tonkinesecatclub.co.uk)

This is mainly for those residing in the UK. Membership of the club includes Tonkinese cat breeders and exhibitors from different parts of UK.

Tonkinese Breed Club (www.tonkinese.info)

This is another Tonkinese cat club that is best suited for those living in the UK. It draws members from Tonkinese cat breeders and exhibitors from across the UK.

What age to buy and Why

This is one of the important decisions you need to make long before you visit a cat breeder with the aim of buying a Tonkinese kitten or cat. The age of your children in case you have children at home is very critical. Although the cats are generally fond of children, having young children at home may make it necessary for you to buy one aged two years and above. This will be a cat capable of understanding children.

Being a senior citizen makes it necessary to avoid buying a Tonkinese kitten at all costs. This is because kittens can be very mischievous and troublesome. They need constant watch, a task you may not be comfortable performing. You may therefore need to buy one aged at least two years. Note that buying a much older cat may not be appropriate considering the fact that an old cat is already used to a specific routine and behaviour.

How much time you plan to spend with your cat is also a very important factor to consider. Buy a Tonkinese cat aged at least three years in case you will not be at home all the time, unless you plan to have someone at home on a regular basis.

You may consider buying a Tonkinese kitten if you take into consideration the element of training. Although there are Tonkinese cat breeders who sell off kittens as young as four or six weeks, the breed's kittens are better separated from their mothers when they are at least 12 weeks. Although a kitten you buy will have received some level of basic training, you will still have the opportunity to offer the kind of training that suits your home and your preference.

One challenge that you may face when you buy a kitten is in determining its personality. The fact that you are not in a position to determine a kitten's personality at such a tender age may make it necessary to buy a young but mature Tonk.

One or More and Why

The decision on whether to buy one, two or more Tonkinese kittens or cats depends on several factors, one of which is resources. You may opt to buy two cats if you are financially capable of meeting their feeding, care, grooming and health needs. You also need to consider the amount of space you have in your house. Although you may be comfortable with only one, it would be ideal if you could buy two for their own companionship.

Male or Female and Why

Different people have different preferences when it comes to the gender of a pet they plan to buy and the same applies to buying a Tonkinese cat. While there are those who prefer male cats, there are also those comfortable with female cats.

The most important thing to note is that whether you choose to buy a male or a female Tonkinese cat, each gender has its pros and cons. Like with other male cats of other breeds, a male Tonkinese cat will roam in search of a female to mate with. Males also tend to mark their territory, which in the case of the Tonkinese breed is inside the house, which creates an environment where catfights may be the order of the day when you introduce another male cat or a different pet. Even though Tonkinese cats are known to be very receptive to other breeds of cats and pets, you cannot rule out chances of catfights.

Likewise, a female Tonkinese cat will also roam in search of a mating partner when on heat. Note that just like with other female breeds of cats, a female Tonkinese cat will come on heat regularly until such a time that it finds a mate, a period that can last up to 16 days. Female Tonkinese cats usually become sexually mature once they attain the age of between eight and ten months and you may not find it comfortable living with a female on heat considering that she will keep on calling day and night.

Such problems should not in any way deter you from owning either gender of a Tonkinese cat. You can have your kitten or adult cat de-sexed before you bring him/her home. De-sexing is the procedure where cats and other animals are subjected to surgical routines that make them incapable of reproducing. De-sexing literally kills their sex drive. While de-sexing in male animals is professionally known as neutering, it is spaying for female animals.

Neutering/Spaying

Neutering in male animals including male Tonkinese cats involves removal of the testes. This renders your cat sterile, which provides for several benefits. On the other hand, spaying in female animals including female Tonkinese cats involves removal of the ovaries and uterus. There are cases where only the ovaries are removed. Like with neutering, spaying also provides for several benefits.

Having your cat neutered or spayed can be beneficial to you in many ways. In addition to being a birth control method, neutering/spaying transforms your cat's general behaviour. A male Tonkinese cat that has been neutered will not only show reduced aggression tendencies; it will also change its mounting and urine spaying behaviour. Likewise, a female Tonkinese cat that has been spayed will show less aggression toward males due to reduction in levels of sex hormones.

One of the biggest advantages of having your Tonkinese cat neutered/spayed is the elimination of roaming. Female cats do produce pheromones into the air when they are on heat. Pheromones are chemical signals that attract male cats for mating. A neutured cat does not react on sensing pheromones in the air and will therefore not roam in search for the cat on heat. On the other hand, a spayed female cat is incapable of releasing pheromones and will therefore not roam in search of a male.

The benefits of having your cat de-sexed are not restricted to behavioural changes. There are health benefits as well. Spaying a female Tonkinese cat relieves it of anxiety and stress she would otherwise have when on heat and denied the opportunity to mate. Note that a female cat on heat can remain in the same state for up to 16 days and is bound to be stressed without an opportunity to mate. The female's condition is even made worse by the fact that it is bound to come on heat again after about 14 days after the initial phase.

Like with other cat breeds, female Tonkinese cats are susceptible to mammary cancer, which is mainly caused by reproduction hormones. Spaying reduces the risk of mammary cancer by between 30 and 50%. Spaying also reduces the risk of such health problems as reproduction tract tumours and other related infections.

Another benefit that de-sexing your cat provides relates to the amount of money you would incur in maintenance. The cost of maintaining a de-sexed cat is relatively lower compared to maintaining a cat that has not been subjected to the same.

When to Have Your Kitten or Cat Neutered/Spayed

There is really no fixed age at which you can have your cat neutered or spayed. You only need to consult your veterinarian to perform the necessary surgical operation. A trend that is now emerging is where breeders offer for sale neutered/spayed kittens and cats, saving you from the cost and the trouble of looking for a veterinarian to perform the procedure.

Tonkinese cat breeders across the world neuter male kittens when they are about six months old. Some breeders neuter them when they are only four weeks old. Likewise, females are spayed when they are between five and eight months. Some breeders spay them when they are only three months of age.

Contrary to a common belief, neutering/spaying kittens at such a tender age does not hinder their overall development. Neutering/spaying kittens is also beneficial since they have the opportunity to heal faster than when de-sexing is performed when they are mature. Apart from breeders, you can have your cat neutered/spayed by your local veterinarian.

Chapter 6 – How to Prepare for Your Tonkinese Cat

What to Know Before You Buy

There are a number of things you need to know before you buy a pet or a Tonkinese cat as a pet for that matter. Knowing some of these things will make living with your cat not only easy but an enjoyable experience as well.

Buying a Tonkinese kitten or cat is similar to introducing a new member into your family. You will be obligated to treat your cat in the same way that you do your family members. You therefore need to be prepared to cater for your cat's needs in terms of food, veterinary care, shelter, grooming and love.

Buying a cat is a life-long commitment. You need to be prepared to live with your cat for a long time. Note that the Tonkinese breed is one of the long-living breeds of cats. Although the breed has an average lifespan of between 15 and 18 years, they can actually live much longer depending on the quality of life you subject them to. It is not surprising that there are Tonkinese cats that have lived to attain the age of 20.

Unlike some other breeds of cats, the Tonkinese breed is an attention seeker. It likes to show off its skills in the presence of family members and visitors. You will therefore need to spend a considerable amount of time with your cat. Furthermore, be prepared to be watched keenly. This is because the Tonkinese cat is very curious and will watch everything that you do and do not be surprised to have a helping hand.

The Tonkinese cat is predominantly an indoor cat. Although it spends most time indoors, it occasionally ventures outdoors not only to play but to explore as well. It is therefore very important that both the indoor and outdoor environments are pet friendly.

Bring your cat home only when everything is in place. Do not bring the cat home before you have enough food supply and other essentials such as bowls and play toys.

Scratching is an innate characteristic of all breeds of cats, the Tonkinese cat included. Ensure that you have a scratch post strategically located for your cat's convenience.

One of the most important things you need to know about the Tonkinese cat is that it will depend on you to a very large extent. Unlike other cats, the Tonkinese cat has thick, soft and silky hair that remains close to the coat. It does not therefore shed heavily.

The most important thing you cannot ignore when you are about to bring your kitten or cat home is to cat-proof your house by establishing a safe room. Cat-proofing your house simply means making your house as secure as possible for the benefit of your cat. This you can do by removing or storing sharp objects that stand out and tucking away wires. A safe room does not necessarily mean a room preserved for the cat. It simply refers to a specific location such as an ideal corner within one of the rooms that your cat will be trained in to get used to as its "home".

Essential Supplies

There is serious need to prepare well long before you bring home your Tonkinese kitten or cat. You will need to invest in a good number of items/equipments for the benefit of your pet. It is very important that you invest in high quality equipment that will serve you for reasonable time. It is not mandatory that you must spend money in buying some of the equipment. There is equipment that you can easily make at home in case you happen to be a DIY person. The following are some of the most essential items that you must have.

Food

Food is the first item that you must have before you bring your kitten or cat home. However, not all foodstuffs will do. You need to buy specially formulated cat food that will allow your cat to grow strong and healthy. It is important to note that cats require specific dietary nutrients and it is only appropriate that you buy foodstuffs that contain such nutrients.

Specially formulated commercial cat foods are readily available from pet food stores and it is recommended that you check at your local pet store outlet for the same.

You will definitely find cat food in different forms. Like with dry foodstuffs, dry cat foods contain limited moisture. They are in most cases sprayed with fat to make them palatable. They also contain added nutrition ingredients to replace vital nutrients destroyed during preparation.

Wet cat food is usually canned or in foil pouch form. There are also fortified vegetarian cat foods. Because cats are obligate carnivores, their vegetarian food is usually fortified with such ingredients as taurine and arachidonic acid, ingredients that cats are not in a position to synthesize from plants.

It is highly recommended that you buy dry, wet and vegan cat food to allow your cat have a complete diet. It is also highly recommended that you buy cat food from reputable stockists who stock cat food brands of good reputation.

Food & Water Dishes

Your cat will definitely eat and it is only appropriate that you buy recommended cat food and water dishes. Just in the same way that you pay attention to the colour and size of your dishes, you need to choose your cat food and water dishes carefully. Doing so will make it possible for your cat to enjoy eating and drinking.

Litter Box & Scoops

By natural instinct, your cat will dig and bury its waste. It is therefore very necessary that you buy an appropriate litter box filled with clean litter. You have the option of buying an open or enclosed litter box. Self-cleaning litter boxes have of late hit the market, which you may also consider buying.

Cat Furniture

Although full of energy and at times very playful, your cat will once in a while want to rest and catch a nap. Investing in a cat condo is therefore very appropriate. Alongside a condo should be a cat tree. A cat tree is very important because your cat will naturally want to scratch in order to sharpen its claws. Having a cat tree will save you from the agony of having your furniture scratched. An alternative to a cat tree is a cat scratching post in case you have limited space.

Cat Carrier

It is very important that you invest in a quality cat carrier. It becomes handy when you need to transport your cat to the vet or when travelling. A quality carrier should have enough room in which you can place a small cat condo.

Brush

Even though the Tonkinese breed of cat does not shed too much hair, you still need to invest in quality brushes for occasional grooming. This will go a long way in preventing the development of hairballs.

Collar

This is one of the most important things you cannot afford not to have when you bring your Tonkinese kitten or cat home. This is because you never know when your cat will venture outdoors with the possibility of getting lost. A collar that you buy should have room for your cat's name, your name and address/contact.

Unlike commonly available collars, you need to invest in a soft collar that will not make your cat uncomfortable.

Non-Essential Supplies

Although generally considered as non-essential cat supplies, some of the following items can be very important especially when you need to have an active, healthy and intelligent Tonkinese cat as a companion.

Tonkinese cats are generally playful, which may make it necessary for you to invest in cat toys. Alternatively, consider using such readily available items as paper bags and cardboards when playing with your cat.

Although your cat will naturally scratch as one way of sharpening/cutting its claws, you may need to consider investing in a cat nail clipper for trimming its claws.

Feeding your cat dry, wet and vegetarian food should be enough to cleanse its teeth. You may however consider buying cat toothbrush and paste just to ensure that you cleanse its teeth well.

Licensing

Bringing a Tonkinese kitten or cat home as a pet is similar to enlarging your family. The breed indeed develops closeness and unique attachment to all family members and considers itself part of the family. This is one of the reasons why you need to license your cat. Licensing your cat is similar to buying insurance cover. Licensing it makes it easy for animal control officers to reach you in case your cat gets lost and is found.

The other reason why you need to license your cat relates to disease control. You give out vital information to animal control officers when you license your cat. Data captured during licensing benefits you in a great way. This is so because you will be contacted in case of newly available vaccinations. More importantly, licensing your cat makes it easy for animal officers, cat breeders and animal health authorities to have vital statistics necessary for planning.

Different countries have different legislations that relate to pets including cats. There are countries where cat owners are not obligated to buy licenses for their cats but are for dogs. There are also countries where licensing is compulsory for all pets. Cat licensing requirements and fees differ across the Unites States of America. While it is mandatory in such states as Los Angeles for dogs to be licensed, licensing is not required for cats.

Likewise, there are states where it is mandatory for cats to be licensed. In addition to licensing, cats must carry proper identification. In such states, licensing is by a country's relevant animal authority. There are also states where veterinarians are given the responsibility of licensing cats. This is so because cat licenses are meant to last for the duration of vaccination. Cat owners therefore find it easy to renew their cat licenses when returning their cats for vaccination.

Cat licensing is mandatory in the UK. In addition, your cat will need to have a cat tag. Cat licensing in the UK is the responsibility of different authorities concerned with the welfare of cats and other pets. However, most licenses are issued by local authorities at the local level. Cat owners can also buy licenses or renew their cat licenses at animal care centers.

It is important that you do not view licensing your cat as a legal requirement. View it as one of the most effective ways of protecting your cat. You also need to consider registering your Tonkinese cat with your local Tonkinese cat club or association if you happen to live in an area with an established cat club or association. This particularly applies in case you live in a jurisdiction where licensing of cats is not mandatory.

Microchipping

Microchipping refers to the latest technology used in identifying lost animals including pets. Unlike externally attached Radio Frequency Identification tags commonly used to identify farm animals, microchipping involves implantation of a small Radio Frequency Identification chip just under a pet's skin.

You can have your Tonkinese cat microchipped. This is a service offered by veterinarians. You will have the chip implanted under your cat's skin at the back of its neck. This is the area with layers of connective tissue capable of holding the chip in place. Although use of microchips is not yet widespread, there are jurisdictions where you are obligated to have your cat or other pet microchipped.

There are several benefits that you derive from having your cat microchipped. From the onset, it becomes easy for animal control officers and animal shelter organizations to contact you in case your cat gets lost and is found. Having your cat microchipped is also beneficial to you considering the fact that cat or pet registries, veterinarians and trainers use microchips to identify pets under their care.

Microchipping is very important and it is not surprising that many breeders including Tonkinese cat breeders microchip their kitten/cats before selling them off. The chip contains all the information that you provide including your name, residence and contact information.

Introducing Your Kitten/Cat to Your Home

Just in the same way that you take time to get used to a new environment, your cat will take some time to get used to your home. Your cat may not behave in a way you expect during the first few days. It will certainly not eat and behave as you expect.

Like with any breed of cat, the Tonkinese breed is a territorial animal. This is why it is very important that you designate for it a room or space in your house. Your cat will naturally spend the first few days or weeks learning every sound and smell in its territory before venturing into other rooms. One of the most important things that your cat will learn is your body language and the tone of your voice. It is therefore very important that you take all these into account when communicating with your cat.

Your main task during the first few days should be to introduce your cat to its important tools. This is the time to introduce it to its litter box, feeding dishes, water dishes and furniture including a scratching post. Tonkinese cats are very intelligent and therefore learn very fast. They follow minor instructions to the letter. This is also the right time to introduce one or two toys for play.

Introducing toys will make your cat get involved in play activities, which will go a long way in eliminating boredom. You will need to spend the first few days observing your cat with the aim of ascertaining its demands, which you will need to fulfill. The main point here is to make your cat feel as comfortable as possible. One thing you are most likely to observe is its act of hissing and growling at any new sound or movement. This is normal and should not be a concern.

Introducing Your Kitten/Cat to other Pets

Although Tonkinese cats are generally receptive to other breed of cats and other pets, bringing your cat home when you already have other pets and in particular another cat can be a serious challenge. This is so because the resident cat already considers your home its territory and will not welcome another cat very easily. Because your Tonkinese cat may not present a problem, the challenge may be how to deal with the other cat or pet. To prevent such a scenario, it is always recommended that a cat you introduce should be of the opposite sex of the resident cat. Note that you will not be able to prevent catfights even when both of them are de-sexed.

The easiest way to introduce your Tonkinese cat to other cat(s) and pets is to set them apart. You need to create a separate room or space for your new cat and let them bond naturally. Bringing in a new cat and housing them in the same room or space can be very problematic.

Introducing Your Kitten/Cat to Family Members

Introducing your cat to family members and in particular to children the first time you bring it home is not recommended. Doing so can be stressful to the cat. It can actually feel very uncomfortable and take very long to get used to its new environment.

When to introduce your cat to family members depends on how fast it has gotten used to its room or space. While some cats take between two and four weeks to get accustomed and start interacting with family members, others take as little as a few days.

It is recommended that you do not introduce your cat to several family members at the same time. Only one family member should venture into the cat's room or space with the aim of bonding with the cat. For easy bonding, a family member venturing into the cat's room or space should not stand but rather sit on the floor when communicating with the cat. Light touch is recommended for the cat to get used to the family member and build trust. Tonkinese cats are generally inquisitive and will naturally walk slowly toward a family member they are not used to. It is therefore very important that a family member who ventures into the cat's room or space for the first time keeps his/her distance and let the cat walk towards him/her.

One rule of thumb that any new family member venturing into a cat's room or space for the first time is to avoid picking up the cat. Although Tonkinese cats are generally lap cats, it is not recommended that they be picked up by those they are not used to. They however choose when to leap onto one's lap. Even so, a family member interacting with the cat for the first time should avoid picking up the cat. Family members also need to note that there are times when the cat will want to have its peace and will show this by hiding underneath its furniture or bed. It should simply be left alone when this happens.

There are several ways through which you can introduce your cat to other family members quickly. The first of these is for a family member venturing into the cat's room or space to engage the cat in play activities with the use of toys. Bringing the cat small amounts of food is also another great way for your cat to bond with other family members.

Although Tonkinese cats get along well with other pets including dogs, it can still be challenge to bring a Tonkinese cat to a home with a dog as another pet. It is always a good idea to keep your cat indoors in its room or space before you allow it to venture into other rooms or outdoors. Even so, it will be beneficial to keep the dog on a leash to allow the cat to explore its new surroundings. You will need to give your cat room to approach the dog on its own terms. Because your cat will naturally approach the dog to sniff it, you will need to be prepared to act when necessary, just in case the dog is not welcoming. The first few days or weeks upon bringing your cat home will be very involving and challenging. It is therefore very important that you create enough time to be at home most of the time to ensure that your cat remains comfortable as much as possible. The challenge eventually wears off once the cat gets used to its new environment, family members and other pets in the home.

Mistakes to Avoid

There are several serious mistakes that most new cat owners do that you need to avoid at all costs. Avoiding these mistakes goes a long way in helping your cat get used to its new environment fast enough.

One of the serious mistakes you need to avoid is to fail to make your home pet-friendly. You need to make your home pet-friendly by ensuring that all that your cat will need is in place before you bring it home. Create for your cat a special room or space. You also need to equip the room or space with all that the cat will need. These include litter box, cat furniture and food/water dishes among other vital equipment.

Tonkinese cats are people-oriented cats and one of the costly mistakes you need to avoid is to leave your cat alone for lengthy periods of time. Leaving your cat alone for a long time can easily drive it into developing a feeling of loneliness, increased anxiety and undesired behaviour. Make it a point to have someone at home most of the time, as your cat will need companionship.

Tonkinese cats are clever and highly intelligent cats. They are very receptive to training, which you need to embark on as early as possible. Although certain training aspects will definitely require a professional trainer, teaching your Tonkinese cat obedience commands should not be a problem. Ensure that your cat can positively respond to such minor commands as sit, stay and leave. A cat that follows commands will rarely develop untoward behaviour.

Every home has rules that family members are obligated to stick to and your home is no exception. As part of your family, do not fail to make your cat aware of simple rules particularly when it comes to feeding time. It can not only be embarrassing but injurious for your cat to pounce on your hands when presenting it with food. You need to avoid such behaviour by getting your cat used to sitting before feeding. This is something that the rest of your family members must be aware of.

Another serious mistake you need to avoid is to give your cat too many treats. While treats are an effective way of rewarding your cat whenever it does something positive such as following instructions, giving too many treats negates the value of training.

You need to use treats sparingly. Restrict dispensing of treats to those occasions when your cat does something extra. One of the costly mistakes that new cat owners make is neglecting to socialize with their pets as much as possible. Like with dogs, failure to socialize with your cat makes it fearful and can easily develop into aggressive behaviour. It is therefore appropriate to introduce your cat not only to family members but to your visitors as well.

Tonkinese cats are strictly indoor cats. Although they occasionally venture outdoors for play, they spend most of their time indoors. One of the mistakes you need to avoid is to restrict your cat indoors. It is always good to take your cat out for walks, giving it an opportunity to climb trees, which is in its nature. Doing so allows your cat to release pent-up energy that it would otherwise channel into undesirable behaviour. A common mistake that most cat owners commit that you also need to avoid is failure to keep their cats mentally active. Many cat owners limit themselves to socializing with their cats, forgetting that keeping their cats mentally active is also beneficial. Like with other pets, cats kept without mental activity become easily bored. Engage in play activities using cat toys. Hide such toys and let your cat find them, for example.

To those who have owned the Tonkinese cat; it is a very adorable cat, which makes many of their owners commit one serious mistake; failure to punish their cats when they engage in untoward behavior. Because physical punishment is likely to instill fear in your cat, consider using a harsh tone when communicating and expressing your disapproval for a behavior that does not impress you.

These are just a few of the mistakes you need to avoid if you need to have a well-behaved and obedient Tonkinese cat as a pet. Failure on your part will simply mean having a pet that you cannot control, which will be a recipe for serious problems at home.

Chapter 7 – Care for Your Tonkinese Cat

Basic Care

Like with all cats, your Tonkinese cat depends on you for everything including basic care. Although your cat is independent to some extent, you are still obligated to provide it with suitable and healthy food, shelter, veterinary care, training and love. It is only with appropriate basic care that you can be able to develop a strong and rewarding relationship with your cat.

Apart from such necessities as food and shelter, proper hygiene is mandatory as part of basic care. Your Tonkinese cat in particular needs to be in a clean environment at all times. Do ensure that all equipment including litter box, food/water dishes, playing toys and the room remain clean all the time. Cats are generally clean pets and do not be surprised when your cat avoids the litter box, feeding and its room when you fail to maintain good hygiene standards. Basic care also involves your cat's safety. Being an indoor cat, you need to know where your cat is at all times.

Just in the same away that you and your family members visit your physician for regular check-ups, your cat also needs to visit a vet for regular check-ups. You do not need to wait for your cat to show signs of illness to take it to a vet. It is during such check-ups that minor signs of illnesses can be diagnosed and proper treatment administered. This is one of the most important basic care routines that you cannot ignore when you need to have a healthy Tonkinese cat as a pet.

Closely related to regular check-ups is feeding. Failure to feed your cat on nutritious food can easily lead to cat medical problems. You need to avoid the practice by some cat owners who feed their cats on dog food. Cat nutritional requirements differ in a big way from dog nutrition needs and feeding your cat on dog food simply denies your cat vital nutritional supplies.

Grooming is a very important part of your cat's basic care. However, your Tonkinese cat does not shed heavily and you will only need to groom it occasionally. In addition to grooming, you also need to clip your cat's claws.

Training your cat is a very important part of basic care. By their nature, cats generally know how to do their own things, which, regrettably, may not be proper. Training your cat from the earliest opportunity goes a long way in preventing such habits as jumping on the kitchen counter, scratching the couch and eating plants. Note that it is through training that your cat comes to learn about applicable house rules.

Although cats generally know how to entertain themselves, a Tonkinese cat in particular can be very playful and destructive when bored. It is therefore very important that you regularly engage your cat in play activities by use of cat toys and other suitable items. Engaging your cat in play activities provides for valuable benefits including strengthening your relationship. Furthermore, playing with your cat on a regular basis provides it with both the physical strength and mental stimulation it so much needs.

There is nothing as great and valuable as giving your cat proper basic care right from the time you bring it home. Giving your cat basic care can indeed be beneficial to you since you will prevent common cat diseases that can otherwise be costly when you have to take your cat to a vet for treatment. It is also by giving your cat proper basic care that you get to have a well-behaved cat at home as a pet.

Living Quarters

Your cat's living quarters are its most important location. Although your cat obviously ventures into other rooms and in particular the living room, there are times when it will naturally retreat back to its living quarters. This is usually the time when it needs to catch a nap or simply relax. This makes it very important to know how to treat its living quarters.

Whether you have enough room at home and have designated a room for your cat or just created a special place in one of the rooms as your cat's living quarters, the room or space needs to be as clean as possible. You need to maintain cleanliness in the room or space as much as possible to make your cat feel comfortable. That cleanliness extends to ensuring that the litter box(s) and everything else in the room or space remains clean.

Just in the same way that you arrange your rooms in the best way possible, you need to ensure that your cat's living quarters is properly arranged. Do ensure that the litter box is far away from feeding/water dishes. The scratching post should also be strategically located for your cat to find it easy to perform its scratching ritual.

Grooming

"The only self-cleaning thing in this house is the cat". This is a very common phrase used on many refrigerator magnets and for good reason. By their nature, cats are the epitome of cleanliness and will go to great lengths to ensure that they remain clean at all times. This is why you observe your Tonkinese cat "licking" parts of the body with the tongue.

The "licking" is not actually licking. It is actually a means through which your cat cleans itself, using the tongue as a washcloth. Cats generally have a unique tongue; it is barbed, making it useful for a good number of purposes. It uses its tongue as grooming tool, using it to remove loose fur, in stripping away scent of food, in getting rid of such parasites as fleas, for increasing blood circulation and for controlling its body temperature. Your cat naturally applies saliva on its forepaw before embarking on the grooming routine.

The onset of self-grooming starts right when a cat is born. The mother naturally "licks" its kittens to not only keep them clean but to also arouse them to suckle, to stimulate them to remove body waste (feces and urine) and to provide them with comfort, especially when it is hot. For the kittens, self-grooming starts when they are about four weeks old.

It is very important to know how your cat grooms itself to enable you to know how you will groom it. When self-grooming, your cat applies saliva to the inside part of one paw before cleaning itself in an upward circular pattern. It naturally starts by cleaning its nose before proceeding to the eyes, backside of the ears and eventually the forehead. Your cat does the same with the other paw. It is only after this that your cat embarks on grooming such other parts of the body as its front legs, shoulders, flanks, genital area, hind legs and the tail. This can be a time-consuming exercise, which can last for an hour.

The importance that cats in general attach to self-grooming makes it very necessary that you too groom your cat. Indeed, the Tonkinese cat, just like other cat breeds, does enjoy grooming. Grooming your cat does not only make it clean, doing so also goes a long way in developing a strong bond between you and your cat in addition to allowing you to screen for any visible skin problems.

Ensuring that your cat's ears and eyes are clean through grooming is very important. You need to examine your cat's eyes and ears for any signs of debris that you need to clean out to prevent build up. The ears are in particular prone to build up of wax that you need to remove frequently. You need to invest in an ear lobe and cotton balls that are effective in cleaning both the eyes and ears.

You however need to be careful when cleaning your cat's ears. Restrict yourself to cleaning visible areas only.

Although your cat naturally indulges in its natural habit of scratching at the scratching post, you still need to examine its nails to ensure that they remain as short as possible. Make it a habit to trim your cat's nails only once in a month using a quality clipper. One area you need to avoid reaching when clipping is the triangular area of the paw that is usually pink in colour. Referred to as the quick, cutting into this area leads to bleeding, which can make it very difficult to clip your cat's nails next time since it will naturally develop fear.

It is important to note that you only need to clip the front paws. The hind paws rarely grow long. Unlike most cat breeds, the Tonkinese cat breed loves water and bathing. It is therefore appropriate to bathe your cat at least twice a week. It is during bathing that you can easily remove any mats that start developing. You need to invest in quality medicated soap, shampoo and conditioning for bathing.

Grooming Products

There are a good number of cat grooming tools on the market that you need to invest in to make your cat clean, healthy and comfortable. These include brushes, flea/tick combs, sprays, shampoos, conditioners, clippers, scissors and lint removal tools. Some of the notable brands include Andis, Bio-Groom, Evercare and Oyster among other brands.

Although ignored by some cat owners, taking time to groom your Tonkinese cat is very important. You need to set apart at least an hour once a week to groom your cat. This is particularly important considering that your Tonkinese cat has thick hair that can easily develop hairballs when not groomed.

Transportation

Cats and Tonkinese cats in particular make valuable pets. Not only are they adorable and make good companions; they also cheer you up when you are down in addition to making you remain active as you engage them in play. Unlike other breeds of cats that are not fond of travelling, Tonkinese cats are very outgoing and love new environments so long as they are protected from adverse weather conditions. You however need to note that travelling with your cat in a car can make it very uncomfortable and most likely to vomit, pee and possibly get dehydrated, which can make your journey a very disappointing one.

You need to invest in a quality cat carrier in order to transport your cat without any problems. A carrier you buy should be spacious enough to allow your cat to stand, turn around and stretch. It should also be very warm and comfortable. The best way to transport your cat using a carrier is to have your cat get used to it several days before you travel.

As part of transport preparation, it is recommended that you consult with your vet for appropriate transport advice especially when you plan to travel with your cat over a long distance. Your vet will be able to prescribe medications and sprays that will calm your cat during the journey, in effect eliminating stress, which affects cats when being transported.

Food usually plays a major role in the comfort of a cat when travelling in a car. Your cat is most likely to vomit if you feed it just minutes before you embark on a journey. It is recommended that you feed your cat at least two hours before you set off to prevent vomiting. One serious mistake you need to avoid when travelling with your cat in a car is to let it out when you stop along the way. Your cat will become confused and possibly run away. Only let it out if you have a leash.

Exercises

Tonkinese cats make very good indoor pets. This makes it very necessary that you subject your cat to different exercises. Depending on the type of food, how frequently you feed it and the kind of treats you give it, your cat can easily gain excess body weight, which is a foundation for serious health conditions.

The only effective way to help your cat in maintaining a healthy body weight is through exercise. Exercising your cat is also beneficial even if it does not gain excess body weight. Exercising your cat goes a long way in ensuring that it remains physically fit.

By their nature, Tonkinese cats are very flexible animals and can perform different types of exercises. One of the simple exercises you may consider subjecting your cat to is by use of a laser pointer. Moving the laser around at different heights gives your cat a good opportunity to stretch as it moves to paw the light on a wall.

You definitely cannot ignore the importance of a cat tree when it comes to exercising your cat. Having a cat tree gives your cat a good opportunity to exercise as it climbs it. The other benefit of having a cat tree lies in the fact that you do not need to be around for your cat to exercise; it can do so even in your absence on its own. In absence of a cat tree, you need to ensure that there are no obstructions to windows to allow your cat to jump on the windows as it pleases.

Having plenty of cat toys is beneficial to your cat in terms of exercise. Because of their playful nature, you need to have different types of cat toys that allow for different types of exercise. You may alternatively use readily available items at home instead of buying.

Many cat owners have of late found their treadmill valuable in exercising their cats and you too may consider the same if you happen to have one at home. Although your cat will learn quickly on how to walk and run on the mill, you will need to supervise it very closely.

One form of exercise you cannot ignore is taking your cat out for walks occasionally. A simple walk along the road or in a park exposes your cat to a new environment, which in itself provides for additional psychological benefits.

Cat Toys

Ensuring that your cat exercises on a regular basis is very important and there is no better way to do so than with cat toys. Cat toys provide the opportunity for your cat to exercise both body and mind. Not only does your cat's body remain physically fit; its mental health is also enhanced, in the process relieving stress in addition to improving blood circulation within the body. Cat toys are also very effective in training a cat to abandon retrogressive behavior while at the same time acquiring progressive behavior.

There are basically four types of cat toys that you need to invest in:

Wand Toys

A wand toy does not need to be a special item. You can make use of a stick or a piece of cloth. Twitching (stick) or waving (cloth) in circles has the positive effect of enticing your cat. This is because such an item's movement becomes similar to a potential prey. You can add other enticing items on the wand to make it not only attractive but also encouraging for your cat to keep on playing. Such other items you can add on the wand include coloured feathers.

It is very important that you keep the wand away from the cat once play session is over. Your cat should not get used to the wand because that may negate its usefulness during play. It will be similar to a cat getting used to a prey to a point that it does nothing when the prey passes by. There are different wand brands on the market if you choose to buy.

Ball Toys
Balls are very effective as cat toys. Unlike ordinary balls however, cat ball toys are small. To your cat, the movement of these balls on the floor resembles scampering of potential prey, which entices your cat to a point that it chases after the balls. Like with a wand toy, a good way to effectively make use of cat balls is to add some niceties on the balls, niceties that your cat will strive to chase and grab. You have the option of buying ping-pong balls, sponge balls or Mylar balls among other balls.

Food-Dispensing Toys
These are the best toys to have when you plan to leave your cat at home for a long time in any given day. These toys literally deliver the food to your cat whenever it engages in play with them. One great benefit of these toys is that they teach your cat to work for its food, with the work being the play activity. This engages its mind, teaching it new tricks in the process. You can indeed make use of cat treats with these toys. Like with the other toys, there are different brands of food dispensing ball toys on the market you can choose from.

Catnip Toys
Catnip is a stimulating herb that cats really enjoy eating. Catnip toys are designed in such a way that they allow you to stuff catnip in them. The amount of catnip you stuff in is very critical because your cat can be over-stimulated.

Regardless of which cat toys you decide to buy, the toys should be those that stimulate your cat's natural instincts. The toys should mimic prey to encourage your cat to not only engage in play more but also master requisite intended techniques or behaviour.

Caring for a Pregnant Tonkinese Cat

Although you have the option of buying a spayed Tonkinese kitten/cat, you may also choose to buy one not subjected to the procedure, in which case it is bound to become pregnant when a partner is available or when you take it to a vet for that specific purpose. Caring for a pregnant Tonkinese cat, just like with caring for any pregnant cat, differs greatly from caring for a non-pregnant cat in many respects.

From the onset, you need to know whether or not your cat has attained pregnancy. This should be at the earliest possible opportunity so that you adjust a number of things to suit its condition. Generally, a cat's gestation period ranges between 60 and 70 weeks and although you are not able to ascertain whether or not your cat is pregnant through urine or blood tests, there are specific signs you need to be on the lookout for.

The first sign of a cat's pregnancy is what is usually referred to as pinking up. This is the enlargement of a cat's nipples in which case the nipples not only become enlarged but become pinkish in colour as well. You are able to notice this when your cat is about three weeks pregnant.

Like in human females, pregnant cats gain weight naturally when pregnant. You will notice a gradual increase in body weight when you hold your cat and notice the pregnancy if you are keen. Increase in body weight usually occurs at the same time when pinking up occurs.

Another simple and clear sign of cat pregnancy that can help you know whether or not your cat is pregnant is morning sickness, just in the same way it happens to human females when they attain pregnancy. A clear sign of morning sickness in cats manifests in excessive sleep especially during the morning hours and failure to eat or avoiding certain food.

It is important that you take your cat to a vet for confirmation of pregnancy. A vet will be able to professionally ascertain your cat's pregnancy through palpitation. Even so, this will only be possible when the pregnancy is around four weeks. A vet may also opt to do an ultrasound but not X-ray in ascertaining pregnancy.

With your cat's pregnancy confirmed, you need to quickly adjust several things. Your vet should indeed be in a position to inform you on which adjustments you need to carry out, one of which is nutrition. Your pregnant cat will need increased amount of nutritious food. The amount of food should however not be excessive so as to prevent labour problems when the time comes for her to give birth.

This is also the time to ensure that your cat has access to safe drinking water at all times. You also need to allow your cat have as much rest as possible. She should only be engaged in play when she initiates it. Your cat requires close monitoring during the whole period of pregnancy. Your vet will most likely advise you on when to take your cat for check-ups.

Apart from nutritious food, water and visits to the vet for check-ups, you need to buy several equipment and supplies in readiness for your cat giving birth. These include a kitten box, surgical gloves, syringe/eyedropper to aspirate nose/mouth secretions, cotton thread for ties, scissors, clean towels, antiseptic for cleaning umbilical and kitten milk replacer.

The last week of your cat's pregnancy is a very critical moment. This should be when you have introduced her to the kitten box, which you need to place in a quiet, warm location away from children. Because your cat is most likely to spend much time in her new location, you need to make food and water readily available.

There are a number of things you will notice when your cat will have gone into labour. First, her mammary glands will have increased tremendously in size. She will also most likely start nesting and have a general change in behaviour.

Although you have made every effort to provide your cat with a kitten box, it can occur that your cat chooses to give birth elsewhere but within the house. This is perfectly normal and should not be a cause of concern. You will only need to transfer her and the kittens to the kitten box.

It is natural that your cat will give birth without your help. You do however need to watch her very closely. There are several scenarios that will require that you call the vet since such may turn out to be emergency situations. These include excessive high body temperature, unpleasant smell of discharge, contractions lasting more than 20 minutes without any signs of kitten and protrusion of placenta through the vulva without any sign of kitten.

Taking care of the kitten should not be a big problem since your cat will do almost everything. You will however have specific responsibilities towards your cat. In addition to ensuring that you maintain high level of hygiene in your cat's room or space, you will need to ensure that your cat receives a nutritious diet and supplements to properly feed the kittens. The kittens will be able to start feeding on solid food when they are between four and five weeks, with introduction of solid food being on a gradual basis.

It is only after 12 weeks that you can start weaning the kittens in readiness to selling them off or giving them off as gifts if you so wish. Tonkinese cats are very social animals and it is very necessary that you socialize the kittens as much as possible. Tonkinese cats develop very slowly and the period between six months and two years is particularly very important. This is the time the kittens need to be socialized, which can be by exposing them to your family members and letting them explore other spaces and rooms in the house.

One of the most important things you cannot ignore once your cat gives birth is the need to have the kittens wormed and vaccinated. Your vet should be in a good position to advise you on when this should be done.

It is important to point out that although your cat can take between eight and ten weeks to become pregnant again, the possibility that she can attain another pregnancy at two weeks after giving birth remains high. This is one of the reasons why many cat owners choose to have their female cats spayed. You will therefore need to take precautions to prevent your cat falling pregnant again soon after giving birth, unless you intend it to be so.

One serious challenge you may face once your cat gives birth is when your cat rejects her kittens. This can be very challenging since you will have the responsibility of hand raising the kittens. Generally, Tonkinese cats give birth to few kittens, in most cases between two and five.

Chapter 8 – Feeding

Nutrition

Your cat requires appropriate nutrients necessary for body development, growth and general function of the body. These nutrients reside in the food that you feed your cat on. Failure to feed your cat on nutritious food definitely leads to specific nutrient-deficiency illnesses/diseases, some that are obviously life threatening.

Just in the same way that you pay close attention to what you eat, you also need to pay close attention to what you feed your cat on and in particular when it comes to food composition, which informs the nutritional value of the food.

Of all nutrients, water is probably the most important nutrient that your cat needs, although it cannot survive on water alone. The fact that a big percentage of your cat's body weight is made up of water makes it very necessary that you supply your cat with fresh drinking water on a daily basis. Lack of water in the body does not only interfere with smooth metabolism; it can also be a cause of serious illnesses.

Your cat also needs a sufficient amount of protein. Protein plays a very important role in the body and in particular in the formation of body cells, tissues, enzymes, organs, antibodies and hormones. Your cat's body also requires protein for the repair of body tissues and proper maintenance of the body.

Closely related to protein are amino acids. Amino acids are the building blocks of proteins and while your cat's body can easily synthesize non-essential amino acids from its diet, its body cannot naturally synthesize such essential amino acids as taurine, which makes it necessary for your cat's food to contain this.

Your cat does not only require water and protein. It also requires fats. Fats are very important when it comes to the production of specific hormones and in cell structure. Fats are also required by the body for proper utilization of certain vitamins. The food you feed your cat on must contain such essential fats as linoleic and arachidonic acids. Lack of these fats can easily lead to your cat suffering from reduced growth and skin problems.

As has already been indicated, Tonkinese cats are very playful and therefore require a lot of energy to remain active. This is why you need to feed your Tonkinese cat on carbohydrates. Carbohydrates do not only provide your cat's body with the energy it requires; carbohydrates play a critical role in maintaining the good health of the intestine. You however need to note that cats are generally carnivorous animals and therefore need very little amount of carbohydrates.

Vitamins are the other very important nutrients that your cat needs. Different vitamins play different roles in the body with some vitamins required for enzyme reaction. Since your cat's body cannot synthesize most vitamins, it is very necessary that the food you feed your cat on contains all the required vitamins. Like with the other nutrients, lack of vitamins leads to the occurrence of various vitamin-deficiency illnesses.

Lastly, your cat requires a sufficient supply of minerals for proper bone and teeth development, for metabolic processes and for maintenance of appropriate fluid balance within the body. Because your cat's body cannot synthesize minerals, you must ensure that your cat food contains these vital inorganic compounds.

Although your cat definitely needs different nutrients to grow and remain healthy, the amount of nutrients you feed your cat is very critical. This is so because cats require different amounts of nutrients depending on their age. Tonkinese cats in particular require to be fed on premium food.

Kitten Nutrition

You definitely have no role to play when it comes to feeding kitten with nutrients. Kittens obtain all the nutrients they need for their first few weeks from their mother's milk, which contains all the necessary nutrients. There are instances where the kitten's mother may not be around because of death, illness or when the mother rejects her kittens upon giving birth. In such instance, formulated commercial milk is always the best option.

Unlike some cat breed kittens, the growth of Tonkinese cat kittens is average; neither slow nor fast. The commercial milk you buy must therefore contain adequate amounts of all the nutrients in balanced quantities. It is important to point out that kittens do require energy three times that of adult cats and proteins two times that of adult cats.

Adult Cat Nutritional Needs

Meeting the nutritional needs of an adult cat can be a serious challenge. Not only should an adult cat have enough to eat but also consume a diet rich in all the necessary nutrients. An adult Tonkinese cat is not only active and therefore requires increased amount of energy; it also requires increased amount of protein to repair body tissues and for other body functions as well. It also requires increased amount of essential fats particularly during cold weather. Although it is very necessary that you feed your cat on these, you need to be careful so as not to make your cat obese.

It is very important to note that although your adult cat will need the same amount of nutrients during adulthood, there are exceptions. Periods when your cat is sick or pregnant will definitely raise the need to buy food containing the amount of nutrients necessary taking into account your cat's condition.

Old Cat Nutritional Needs

Just in the same way that feeding kittens and adult cats differ, feeding an old cat also differs. You are most likely to start noticing your Tonkinese cat's aging signs when it is about fifteen years. Because of the body changes, metabolic and immunologic changes it is bound to go through, occurrence of such age-related diseases/health conditions as loss of muscle mass, arthritis, obesity and dental problems among others become common.

Taking into account the changes in an old cat's body and the likelihood of development of the indicated diseases/health conditions, a diet for an old cat should be one that promotes good health and appropriate body weight. Such a diet should ideally be low on carbohydrates but high on proteins, vitamins, essential fatty acids and minerals.

The Right Food

You have two options when it comes to the right food for your cat; canned and dry food, which at times is referred to as dry kibble. Compared with canned food, dry food has low water content, high on carbohydrates and plant protein. Considering that cats are carnivorous animals, dry kibble is not the right food for your cat.

Although your cat needs foods rich in protein, it is better off with animal-based protein. Feeding your cat plant-based protein derived from vegetables simply has no value to your cat in terms of nutrition. Unlike plant-based protein, animal-based protein contains amino acids, the essential fats that are beneficial to your cat. Canned food contains animal-based protein, making canned food the right food for your cat.

Although canned food cannot be said to be that fresh, dry kibble goes through a lot of processing in addition to being cooked at high temperatures for long times. This does not only lower quality of protein within but also damages other nutrients.

The benefit of canned cat food over dry kibble is also in the amount of water contained. Cats generally do not drink water since their prey in the wild supplies them with enough amount of water. Having a cat at home therefore requires that you feed it on a diet rich in water, which makes moist canned food the right food for your cat.

You have two options when it comes to cat food. The first option is to prepare cat food on your own at home or buy commercial canned foods. It is important to look at these two options to enable you make the right decision when it comes to food for your cat.

Unknown to some cat owners, cats are carnivorous animals and therefore rely on eating raw meat. Whether it is fresh or raw meat is neither here nor there since wild cats kill their prey and may not consume the whole prey in one instance. Cat owners who have a negative view on feeding their cats on raw meat therefore deny their cats what they are actually supposed to eat. A common belief by such cat owners usually has to do with the element of food poisoning.

Unlike us humans who are highly susceptible to food poisoning, cats are not. This is because while the food we eat resides in our intestines for anything between 35 and 55 hours, the food that a cat eats only resides in its intestine for between 12 and 16 hours. This simply means that any harmful bacteria remain within a cat's intestine for a short period of time unlike in humans. The short period of time therefore lowers the risk of food poisoning.

It is therefore perfectly in order to buy raw meat to feed your cat on. Even as you do so, you need to remember that not all raw meat sources are the same in quality. You need to consider buying whole cuts of meat that you can thoroughly clean before feeding your cat on instead of buying pre-ground meats available in supermarkets.

It can be very fulfilling if you opt to prepare its food at home. Even as you do so, it is very important that you do not subject your cat to the same meat source. You seriously need to consider changing meat sources. You have the option of feeding your cat on beef, rabbit meat or chicken among others. You also need to consider adding in some water and recommended supplements.

The second option is to go for commercial cat food and in this case canned cat foods. There is however a serious challenge you are likely to face when shopping for canned cat food; marketing gimmicks or food labels. Some of the food labels you are most likely to come across on canned cat foods include "For Indoor-Only Cat", "Natural", "Premium", "Breed Specific", Veterinarian Recommended" and "Therapeutic Diet" among other labels.

Although they seem very promising, some of the food labels can be very misleading. The reality is that most canned foods with these labels contain wheat, corn, soy and by-products. While wheat, corn and soy definitely have high levels of carbohydrate that your cat does not really need, the by-products happen to be the only source of protein for your cat, which is not appropriate.

The only effective way to overcome the challenge presented by promising yet false food labels is to look at both the composition and ingredients used in making canned cat food when shopping. While the composition part of it refers to the percentage of fat, protein and carbohydrate the cat food contains, ingredients refer to the specific nutrients in the food. You need to pay attention to three important things when it comes to choosing the right canned cat food; it should be food that is high in water content, low in carbohydrates and contain animal-based protein instead of plant-based protein.

It is worth pointing out that mainstream canned cat foods can at times be very expensive, depending on your location. This is because they do contain muscle meat of chicken and turkey among others, which is normally listed as the first ingredient.

Depending on your financial position, you may consider buying canned cat foods that contain by-products. These are normally labeled as "chicken by-products" or "turkey by-products" among others. The fact that they are affordable does not mean that they are of no nutritional value.

Like with all canned foods, canned cat foods do feature preservatives and ascertaining the kind of preservative used in cat food is very important. There are canned cat foods that contain such preservatives as ethoxyguin, BHA and BHT. These are chemicals that have been proved not to be safe when used as preservatives. Although most cat food manufacturers have abandoned the use of such preservatives, you need to check to ensure that canned cat food you are about to buy does not contain the same.

Feeding Program

There is really no uniform cat-feeding program. This is the frequency at which you need to feed your cat. How frequently you feed your Tonkinese kitten, adult cat or an old cat definitely differs. This is because they need to feed at different intervals and in different amounts at every stage of their life. Your home environment and type of food you feed your cat on also informs feeding frequency.

Just like with human babies, kittens need to be fed small amounts of food at regular intervals. This is because their tummies are not yet capable of handling large amounts of food, yet this is the time they need a sufficient amount of various nutrients necessary for growth and development. Tonkinese kittens generally need to be fed at least four meals spread out in any given day.

Unlike kittens that need to eat nutritious food for growth and development, your adult Tonkinese cat needs to eat maintenance food. This is food that does not only aid in further development of the body but in maintaining strong healthy bones and in enhancing the body's immune system. Because it can be difficult to ascertain the amount of food that your adult cat needs, it is better to let it eat until it is satisfied. Two meals in any given day should be enough.

Just in the same way that feeding kittens differs from feeding adult cats, feeding an old Tonkinese cat also differs. Old cats are generally susceptible to various diseases and health conditions that make it necessary to tailor their feeding frequency taking into account any health problems they may have. The same goes for sick kittens and adult cats.

It is important to look at the feeding program for adult cats because such is the cat you are most likely to have. You have two options when it comes to designing a feeding program for your cat. Your first option is to let your cat get used to a free feeding program where you fill its feeding dish with a large amount of food that it can eat when it wishes. Although this program best suits a cat that is often left alone at home for a considerable amount of time, it has its disadvantages. First, you are obligated to buy kibble cat food because fresh food may not last long in the open. Secondly, there is the risk of your cat over-eating and therefore developing obesity.

Your other option is to design a scheduled feeding program where your cat gets used to a specific time when it is served food. This program can be very beneficial considering the fact that you are in a position to control how much food your cat consumes at any given time.

The fact that you have designed a feeding program for your cat should not mean that such a program is permanent. There is always room to alter a program depending on different situations such as when travelling, when your cat is sick, when your cat is pregnant (if a female and not spayed) and when adverse weather changes occur.

Food Allergies

Just like it is with humans, cats too develop different allergies including inhalant, fleabite and food allergies. In the case of food, cats generally develop food allergy when subjected to specific food on a regular basis. Tonkinese cats do develop allergies when they are between two and six years although a few have been noted to develop food allergies as early as when they are five months old and when they are as old as fifteen years old.

Contrary to popular belief, food allergy does not necessarily mean food intolerance. Unlike food intolerance that manifests itself in the form of diarrhea and/or vomiting, a food allergy exhibits real symptoms that may include itchy skin, hair loss and excessive scratching among other symptoms.

The causes of food allergy in cats are usually specific ingredients found in cat foods and in particular in such cat food stuffs as corn, soy, dairy products, wheat and seafood. It is worth noting that these are the same food stuffs found in dry or kibble cat foods.

Determining whether or not your cat suffers from a food allergy can be a very big challenge. This is because food allergy symptoms are in most cases similar to those presented by such cat diseases/health conditions as fleabite allergy and intestinal parasite hypersensitivity. There are however several ways through which you can determine whether or not your cat suffers from food allergy or other diseases, although determination can take some time.

The most effective way through which you can determine whether or not your cat suffers from a food allergy is to undertake a food trial. This means subjecting your cat to a specific type of food for several days while looking out for any allergy symptoms. It is important to note that blood tests are only effective in diagnosing other types of allergies but not food allergies.

There are instances where your cat's food allergy and associated symptoms become serious. This is usually the time to take your cat to a vet for examination and treatment. Your vet will most likely feed your cat fatty acids, steroids and prescribe antihistamines as the first line of treatment. The only effective way of treating food allergy in cats is avoidance of the causative food.

What Not to Feed Your Cat

Food that is edible to you and/or your dog may not be edible to your cat. Feeding your cat on certain food cannot only cause allergies and intoxication, consumption of certain food stuffs can easily lead to your cat going into a coma with increased risk of instant death.

It is perfectly normal to have alcoholic beverages at home so long as you keep them safe and away from your cat. Your cat will definitely be intoxicated when it consumes any food containing alcohol and can easily go into a coma with high chances of dying.

Spices make food very tasty but only for humans. Feeding your cat on spices can cause serious allergic reactions and toxicity, which can lead to death.

Cats are carnivorous animals and therefore do well with meat but not bones. Whether from fish, beef, lamb or poultry, bones are dangerous to your cat. Not only can they cause obstruction; bones can also lacerate your cat's digestive system and cause serious problems.

You should not feed or let your cat feed on such food such as tea, chocolate, coffee and caffeine. These contain caffeine, theophylline and theobromine. These are ingredients that cause vomiting and other health problems in cats.

While both human vitamin and mineral supplements can indeed be healthy, they can be very dangerous when you feed your cat on them. You need to keep all your food supplements far from reach of your cat.

These are just a few foodstuffs that you should not feed your cat on. Although your cat will naturally avoid some of this food, you need to safely keep away those that it can accidentally consume.

Cat Treats

Giving your cat treats occasionally is highly recommended. Contrary to common belief by some cat owners, cat treats are not entirely valueless. Modern cat treats are formulated to encourage good dental, digestive, general and skin health, depending on the type of treat you buy. Note that there are crunchy, dental, soft, catnip/grass and jerky cat treats. You also have the option of buying grain-free, natural or organic cat treats. To enhance their appeal and taste, cat treats are in most cases flavoured. You may choose to buy beef, chicken, vegetarian, turkey, tuna or fish flavoured treats.

Your cat definitely needs the intake of calories that cat treats provide. However, it is very important that you measure the amount of treats you feed your cat on. Because cat treats largely contain calories, they should not make up more than 10% of your cat's calorie intake. Your cat should obtain the remaining 90% from quality nutritious foods.

Like with shopping for canned cat food, it is important that you choose cat treats with utmost care. This is because some information contained on cat treat labels may not be correct. You seriously need to look out for the amount of calories a cat treat food contains before you buy.

When to feed your cat treats is very important. This is because there is an increased risk of your cat developing addiction or a taste for treats instead of its regular food. Because of this, you need to feed your cat treats at special occasions only. Such can be when it does something positive like mastering a rule and excelling in an exercise or training.

Because cat treats basically contain calories, they are not recommended for overweight cats. Feeding your overweight cat treats will simply worsen its condition and increase the risk of serious health conditions. For an overweight cat, go for Catnip/grass treats. Both are cereal grasses and therefore low in calories.

You should be able to find different types of cat treats in the market. There are those that are soft and moist and those that are hard, similar to dry cat food. Your cat will most likely hate dry treats in favour of soft treats. It is always a good idea to balance between the two for your cat to receive all the nutrients it needs for good health.

There are a number of cat treat brands on the market and just like with choosing canned food carefully, you need to choose cat treats carefully. The most important things to look into are the ingredients a treat is composed of. This is very necessary because some cat treats may contain ingredients that may cause allergies.

How you store cat treats you buy is of great importance. The Tonkinese is a very clever cat and will notice when you feed it on treats. It will therefore look for the spot where you store its canned food. It may develop the habit of stealing treats if you fail to store the same in a secure place. The best way to go about storing cat treats is to store themin a different location from where you store its regular food.

Chapter 9 – Training

Cat Training

Cat training refers to the practice of instilling certain values in your cat. It is a wide area that also involves changing some of your cat's natural but unpleasant behaviour. Cat training provides for several benefits not only to you but to your cat as well. A well-trained cat usually has its body and mind well stimulated, which goes a long way in enhancing its overall health. Well-trained cats also exhibit good behaviour especially in the presence of visitors. It is also through training that you build a close relationship with your cat. Failure to give your cat the necessary training can easily turn your cat into a pest instead of a pet.

Cat training requires that you first understand your cat in different respects. Luckily, Tonkinese cats are not only highly intelligent buts also very easy to train and remain obedient. You can easily train your Tonkinese cat to stop doing something or to behave in a certain manner at certain times. Like other animals, cats do learn through experience. Your cat will stop doing something from which it has a bad experience with.

You have two options when it comes to training your cat. You have the option of taking your cat to a dedicated cat or pet training centre, invite a cat or pet trainer to your home or undertake the training on your own. Because taking your cat somewhere else or engaging the service of a trainer involves expenses, you may consider undertaking the training on your own. Training your cat personally can be very fulfilling especially when you see your cat positively responding to your instructions.

One thing you must avoid at all costs when training your cat is punishment. Unlike dogs, cats respond negatively to reprimands

71

and punishments. Punishing or reprimanding your cat for failing to follow given instruction develops fear in your cat, which makes training very difficult. Furthermore, a fearful cat will always try to run away. The secret to training your cat effectively lies in using treats. Rewarding your cat with treats whenever it does something positive or when it responds positively and follows given instructions is the only sure way through which you can give your cat proper training. There are three basic areas where you need to train your cat; house training, behavioural training and trick training.

House Training

Being an indoor cat, you no doubt share almost every room in your home with your Tonkinese cat. Although it tends to spend most of its time in its room/space, it will on a regular basis venture into the other rooms for companionship or to simply explore the other rooms. This makes it necessary to train it properly in different areas.

Litter training is the most important house training that you must give your cat. You must however ensure that the litter box is not only clean at all times but placed in the most appropriate location within the cat's room or space. One reason why cats do avoid their litter box and instead choose to urinate or go for long call in other places in the house is usually due to dirty litter. Note that what may seem clean to you may not necessarily be clean to a cat. You need to get accustomed to changing the litter on a daily basis before you can embark on litter training.

You need to start introducing your cat to its litter box immediately when you bring it home. Although filling the litter box with dry and clean soil will naturally attract the cat when it needs to pee or defecate, you still need to introduce your cat to it. It is highly recommended that you place the litter box away from the cat's sleeping quarters and feeding/water dishes. Apart from litter box training, you need to train your cat on where to sit or lie when in the living room.

Behavioural Training

Behavioural training is probably the most extensive and difficult part of cat training. This is because of the many behavioural changes you need to train your cat to adopt or discard.

Your cat naturally has hunting instinct and will naturally bite or claw your hands when you engage it in play activities. Although this is normal cat behaviour, you need to train your Tonkinese cat to abandon this behaviour. The best way to offer the training is during play sessions where you stop play immediately when it bites or claws. This is also the best time to use treats, denying your cat the same when it engages in biting and clawing.

Your action of stopping to play and denying it treats sends a strong message to the cat that it is out of its unbecoming behaviour that play has not only stopped but it has been denied treats as well. You are most likely to notice change in this behaviour during play sessions that follow when your cat resorts to using its paws instead of teeth and nails during play. This is also the time to effectively make use of treats, rewarding it for not biting and clawing.

Cats do communicate by meowing. Your cat will naturally meow when hungry, when in danger, when in need of a mate (in the case of a non-spayed female cat), to attract your attention or when requesting something. Although perfectly normal, excessive meowing can be a serious problem in the house. Your first reaction to your cat's excessive meowing should be to consult your vet with the aim of ascertaining whether or not your cat suffers from an illness or disease.

It is also important to note that such changes in the house as re-arranging the house can make a cat meow a lot. It is equally important to note that you may be the cause of excessive meowing if you have made your cat develop the habit of meowing by giving it something whenever it meows. The most effective way to train your cat to stop excessive meows is to give something like a treat when it is quiet and denying it the same when it meows.

While having a playful Tonkinese cat as a pet is perfectly in order, in can be a big challenge when you have a hyperactive and playful Tonkinese cat. Your hyperactive cat will indulge in such activities as too much play, hiding things in the house, chasing unseen mice, jumping on and off furniture and in extreme cases stealing.

Cats that do exhibit this behaviour are in most cases hyperactive cats not engaged in play activities and often left alone. The most effective way to get your cat to abandon such behaviour is to provide means such as play activities through which your cat can expend the excess energy. In case of an un-spayed or un-neutered cat, this may also be the right time to have it neutered/spayed.

One of the most misunderstood cat behaviors by many cat owners is a cat's territorial behaviour. Like such other wild cats as Leopards, your Tonkinese cat will naturally mark its territory within the house, which can be every room and items in the house including furniture. Note that cats have a high sense of smell and will detect any foreign smell however light it may be.

Your cat has scent glands located along its tail, on its front paws, either side of its forehead, on its chin and its lips. Its behaviour of rubbing its tail or head on you or anything else in the house is therefore not a way of grooming itself but as a way of marking its territory by picking up smell and leaving its smell on the same.

Although it is natural for your cat to mark its territory, it can be on the extreme. Note that cats engage in this behaviour as one way of guarding themselves from possible threats. The scent they leave behind when marking their territory is meant to serve as a warning to other cats that the area is already occupied. The only effective way to train your cat to abandon this behaviour that at times can be irritating is to socialize with your cat as much as possible. Your cat should never feel threatened in any way.

Having an untrained cat at home as a pet can be very dangerous in a cases where you also have a bird or birds as pets. By their nature, cats have hunting and chasing instincts. Although your cat may not chase after prey, which in such a case is the bird to kill for food, it will chase out of instinct with the aim of tossing the bird around, which can result in serious injuries to the bird. This is predatory behaviour that is very common with both indoor and outdoor cats including Tonkinese cats.

Persistent predatory behaviour stems from the fact that your cat will not have the opportunity to vent out its natural instinct and therefore directs the same to the potential in-house pet. The only effective way to offer predatory training is to have your cat socialize with a potential prey under close watch. Such socialization makes the cat realize that the potential prey is indeed part of the family.

Nocturnal Training

Your Tonkinese cat is naturally a nocturnal animal. It will spend a lot of time sleeping during the day and become active during the night when you are asleep. Its night activities can be very disturbing if you do not offer appropriate training. Your cat will naturally become active from late in the evening to early morning.

Letting your cat get used to this schedule will deny you quality sleep. The most appropriate training you offer should aim at changing its schedule of activities, which you can do by engaging it in play activities during the day instead of letting it sleep. Because changing its schedule can be challenging, you need to go about doing so gradually until it gets used to the new schedule.

Even so, you will still not stop your cat from engaging in night activities albeit to a smaller degree. You therefore still need to make available suitable cat play toys to allow your cat to engage in some activities during the night. You however need to set up the toys away from your bedroom to avoid sleep disruption.

Trick Training

One reason why Tonkinese cats make good companions is the fact that they are receptive to trick training. You can train your Tonkinese cat to do a number of things in the house including ringing the door bell or playing dead.

Dominance Training

A Tonkinese cats' body size is not in any way dominating. Unlike larger and hairy cats, it is independent and can easily defend itself against attacks by other cats to a small degree. It is because of the limited independence that you need to offer your Tonkinese cat dominance training. It is through dominance training that your cat gains the confidence it needs when in the presence of other cats. This training is particularly useful in case you live in an area with many other cats in the neighbourhood and your cat ventures out a lot.

Command Training

This is one of the most important trainings you have to subject your cat to. Your cat should be able to positively respond to such commands as come, roll, go and sit. This training requires a lot of time and patience on your part because your cat will obviously not master all the commands you give in one training session.

Leash Training

Walking on a leash is the other important training you must offer your cat. This is so because you will occasionally take your cat out for walks. Unlike most cat breeds however, the Tonkinese breed is very receptive to walking on a leash. Even so, it is highly recommended that you place the leash near its food dish or other favourite location where it sees it often to get used to it. It pays to only buy a harness specially designed for cats. Such do have the leash attachment located behind the harness and not at the neck.

Training Rules

- Regardless of the type of training, be patient but committed to your cat's training schedule.

- Never resort to punishing your cat in case it fails to perform as expected. Punishing it will make it develop fear and therefore fail to master any training that you offer.

- It pays to embark on training at a slow pace, training a single item for several days before introducing another item.

- Always reward your cat whenever it performs better for encouragement.

- Set a specific training time every day. This will get your cat accustomed to training routine.

Chapter 10 – Health

Tonkinese Cat Health

The Tonkinese breed is one of the healthiest breeds of cat that you can find. This is mainly because it is a human-engineered breed obtained by blending Siamese and Burmese breeds. Although such cross breeding tends to make the offspring highly susceptible to diseases and health conditions from the two bloodlines, the first Tonkinese breeders must be complimented for having done a lot to eradicate hereditary diseases and health conditions that the Tonkinese breed would have inherited from the parent breeds.

Unlike cat breeders of a different breed who have to contend with dealing with many hereditary feline diseases and health conditions, a Tonkinese breeder's focus is in maintaining the breed's points and characteristics. The breeders are now largely engaged in maintaining consistency, quality and adherence to set breed standards.

Even so, the Tonkinese is still susceptible to a few diseases and health conditions. They include the following:

Common Illnesses/Diseases

Gingivitis - Gingivitis is a periodontal disease. It causes inflammation of the gums that turn reddish. Plaque formation also occurs. Plaque is basically a collection of debris, food, dead skin, mucous and bacteria. The gingival surface however remains very smooth. The disease can easily be reversed at the earliest stage through proper dental care.

Without proper dental care, the disease develops further with occurrence of calculus under the gums. Calculus is a mixture of organic matter, carbonate and calcium phosphate. In addition to further development of plaque, the gum surface becomes irregular with some pain in the gums.

As the disease progresses, it forms a narrow space between the teeth and the inner wall of the gum. The bacteria present in this space mutate and release toxins that damage gingival tissue. Occurrence of gingivitis is common not only in cats but also in dogs aged three years and above.

Apart from the swelling and reddishness of the gums, other symptoms of the disease include bad breath. Gingivitis is largely caused by the accumulation of plaque. There are also other risk factors that encourage occurrence of the disease. These include excessive soft food, old age, bad chewing habits, diabetes, breathing through the mouth, crowded teeth and autoimmune disease among other risk factors.

Because of the danger that gingivitis poses to your cat, you need to help your cat in preventing the occurrence of the disease. This you can do by ensuring that your cat's oral health remains at its optimum by brushing its teeth at least twice a week with veterinarian toothpaste or using a finger pad to clean the teeth. This simple action goes a long way in preventing build-up of plaque.

A serious case of gingivitis requires veterinarian attention at the earliest possible time. In addition to physical examination, your vet will, as a matter of routine, try to establish possible causes of the disease, which can be the kind of food you feed your cat on.

There are several ways through which your vet may choose to treat the disease, depending on his/her findings. Your vet may prescribe antibacterial solution for squirting on your cat's teeth to prevent build-up of plaque, prescribe dietary supplements or prescribe specific foods that help in promoting good dental health.

In case of serious gingivitis, your vet may choose to remove baby (deciduous) teeth that may cause teeth overcrowding, which is a cause of the disease or remove particular affected teeth. It is also possible that your vet may choose to only remove plaque and calculus before polishing the tooth surface.

Gingivitis is a serious gum disease that you must not let your cat suffer from. This is so because it reaches a stage where your cat will not be able to chew food properly or even eat due to pain. You will certainly not rule out malnourishment and possible death of your pet.

Familial Amyloidosis - This is not a disease but rather a health condition that affects the liver. It is actually a group of disorders with similar characteristics; abnormal deposition of Amyloid (a fibrous protein) into body tissues. Amyloid occurs as a hard and waxy substance and develops as a result of degeneration of tissue. The disposition interferes with the normal functioning of areas where the protein has reached. Familial Amyloidosis is a hereditary health disorder common in Abyssinian, Burmese and Siamese breeds of cats although it can also affect Tonkinese cats.

Although this is a hereditary disorder, it can also be caused by various factors including chronic infection, inflammation of inner layer of the heart caused by bacterial endocarditis and tumour. The condition presents several symptoms including general body weakness, loss of appetite, excessive thirst and urination, vomiting, enlarged abdomen and swelling of the limbs accompanied by joint pain.

Familial Amyloidosis is not treatable. It is a disorder that impairs the liver, seriously affecting its function and that of other body organs and most cats die from the disease. There are however specific measures that your vet can take to lessen the pain and help prolong your cat's life in case of infection. Your vet may take such measures as blood transfusion (blood change), fluid therapy, diet change and in some cases surgery.

Inflammatory Bowel Disease (IBD) - IBD is a term used to refer to several diseases and health conditions that affect a cat's gastrointestinal tract and whose cause(s) remain largely unknown. One characteristic of all the diseases is that they cause inflammation of the intestines.

Your Tonkinese cat will present several symptoms if affected. Some of these include diarrhoea, signs of depression, flatulence, abdominal pain, general body weakness, bloody stool and distressed hair on the coat.

Diagnosis of IBD is normally through laboratory tests including blood count, biochemistry profile and urinalysis. Although a cure for IBD is not available, a vet will normally institute control measures that include stabilization of body weight, reduction of immune system response and administration of antibiotic medications.

Upper Respiratory Infection – This is a disease that mainly affects Tonkinese kittens. However, the kittens do overcome the disease as they grow. The disease presents such symptoms as sniffing, runny eyes and coughing among other symptoms. Upper respiratory infection is caused by two virus; Calicivirus and Rhinotracheitis virus. These two virus attack the lining of the upper respiratory tract and spread very fast among kittens since it is transmitted through sneezing.

The above are the only health problems that affect the Tonkinese breed. You however need to note that your Tonk will still remain susceptible to several other feline diseases and health conditions affecting other cats in your neighbourhood. They include:

Hypertrophic Cardiomyopathy (HCM) - This is the most serious hereditary disease that affects most cats. The disease causes stiffening of the heart wall, in effect restricting flow of blood. This can lead to instant heart failure. Although the disease presents no symptoms, such symptoms as lethargy, excessive weight loss, labored breathing, excessive heart murmur and lameness in the rear legs should be a cause of concern.

It is important that you take your cat to a vet immediately when you notice any of these symptoms for a proper check-up, diagnosis and treatment.

Spinal Muscular Atrophy (SMA) - This is another hereditary disease that all breeds of cats remain susceptible to. It affects kittens in most cases. While an affected kitten remains normal in other areas of the body, the rear legs show signs of lameness. This is because the disease impairs neurons found within the spinal cord.

Reputable Tonkinese cat breeders do engage vets to carry out tests on their kittens to ascertain the presence of the disease before the kittens are sold off.

Hyperthyroidism - This is an endocrine disorder whose occurrence is directly linked to over-activity of the thyroid gland, which leads to excess levels of specific hormones. These hormones play a very important role in the body; the role of controlling metabolism. Increased levels of these hormones have the negative effect of increasing your cat's heart rate with the possibility of your cat developing heart murmur. Without appropriate treatment, the disease easily causes heart failure, kidney damage, high blood pressure and death.

Your cat will exhibit a number of symptoms when infected. These include diarrhoea, vomiting, behavioural changes, weight loss, increased thirst and urination, body weakness, poor coat condition and rapid heartbeat among other symptoms. These symptoms may not necessarily point at hyperthyroidism because the symptoms are presented by other cat diseases including cat diabetes and renal failure. It is therefore very important that you take your cat to a vet once you notice any of these symptoms.

The fact that hyperthyroidism does not affect specific breeds of cats means that all cats are at risk of suffering from the disease. It mostly affects older cats and dogs. There are two main ways of treating hyperthyroidism. A treatment method a vet chooses depends on your cat's medical condition.

Your vet may choose to prescribe such medications as Tapazole whose action is not to treat but to control the disease. Your cat will however need to use prescribed medication(s) for the rest of its life. There are instances when a vet may choose to undertake surgery with the aim of removing the enlarged thyroid. The other treatment your vet may choose is to implement radioactive iodine treatment, which involves injection of a single dose of radioactive iodine. Iodine has the positive effect of destroying the damaged part of the thyroid while leaving normal thyroid tissues intact.

Although these are some of the most common diseases/health conditions your Tonkinese cat is susceptible to, it also remains susceptible to other general cat diseases/health conditions. Such include:

Kidney Disease - Kidney disease is one disease that is often ignored when looking at cat diseases. All cats regardless of breed are susceptible to kidney disease. The kidney plays the important role of removing waste from the bloodstream in addition to regulating the amount of fluids in the body. Failure by the kidneys to play these vital roles puts a cat's life in serious danger.

Kidney disease presents different symptoms including loss of appetite, frequent vomiting, depression, poor coat appearance and frequent urination or no urination. Kidney disease can be acute or sudden and chronic or long-term. It can be caused by such factors as trauma, surgery, shock, serious blood loss, poison, drugs and infection of the kidneys.

Unlike other cat diseases that present symptoms almost immediately, symptoms associated with kidney disease only appear when a large part of the kidneys is already destroyed. It is therefore very necessary that you take your cat for regular veterinary checkups. .

Retinol Atrophy - Retinal atrophy is a non-treatable hereditary disease common in some cat breeds. The disease is also common in some dog breeds. It is the degeneration of the retina, causing gradual loss of vision, which ends in blindness. The disease presents such symptoms as decreased vision at night, dilated pupils and cataract formation among other symptoms.

Pyruvate Kinase Deficiency - Pyruvate Kinase is an enzyme whose deficiency in your cat's body leads to impairment of red blood cells, greatly reducing the ability of red blood cells to metabolize. The inability of red blood cells to metabolize causes anaemia in addition to other blood issues. Pyruvate Kinase deficiency is very common in such breed of cats as the Somali, Tonkinese, Abyssinian and other short-haired cat breeds including the Tonkinese cat.

Caused by defects in genes acquired at birth, Pyruvate Kinase deficiency presents such symptoms as body weakness, anaemia, jaundice and increased heart rate among other symptoms. This condition is usually addressed through bone marrow transplant, which is the only treatment method available. In addition to being an expensive treatment, it is also life threatening. Most cats that suffer from this condition die by the time they attain four years.

Arthritis - Arthritis refers to negative changes that occur within joints. These changes develop when cartilage that protects different bone joints wear out, causing friction at the joints. The friction causes swelling accompanied by pain. Although the cartilage is supposed to be replaced naturally, arthritis is bound to occur when it wears out faster than it is replaced.

Just like in humans, the onset of arthritis in cats is in advanced age although middleaged cats can also suffer from the condition. The swelling and accompanying pain is usually chronic, which causes a lot of discomfort.

There is no cure for Arthritis. It can only be treated with any treatment that a vet offers, treatment that aims at lessening the pain and swelling that your cat experiences. Treatment needs to be offered at the earliest possible time so as to prevent further loss of cartilage.

Although arthritis is common in such other cat breeds as the Himalayan, Siamese and Persian cat breeds, your Tonkinese cat can suffer from the condition due to such factors as old age, obesity, congenital defects, accidents and infection.

Arthritis has a serious effect on a cat's health. This is because it does not only make a cat uncomfortable but impairs its mobility as well. The condition presents such symptoms as limited activity, stiffness in walking, limping and social withdrawal.

Although your vet will definitely prescribe medication that helps in preventing swelling and managing pain, he/she is likely to recommend the most appropriate diet for your cat as the most effective treatment option. This is because food plays a very important role in your cat's overall health.

Allergic Dermatitis - Allergic dermatitis refers to conditions that affect the skin negatively. These can be caused by such factors as food allergy, parasites, hormonal imbalances and infections. One effective way to prevent allergic dermatitis in your cat is to feed it on food rich in meat-based protein, essential fatty acids and antioxidants.

There are however instances when you may need to take your cat to a vet. This is when the skin is not only rough but has wounds. Your cat's skin should be smooth and soft without any signs of flakes. Hair on the skin should also be evenly spread out.

Diabetes - Just like in humans, cats suffer from diabetes when their metabolic system cannot effectively control the amount of sugar in their blood stream. The main cause of this is usually lack of or limited production of insulin, which is produced in the pancreas. Apart from insufficient amount of insulin, your cat is at risk of developing diabetes in case it is obese, approaching old age, is a male, stressed, poor diet and hormonal imbalances.

Diabetes presents several symptoms including excessive thirst, rapid weight loss, loss of appetite, vomiting, increased urination and general body weakness among other symptoms.

Once diagnosed, your vet may recommend a number of ways to help your cat cope. One of the most effective ways your vet is most likely to recommend is diet, the kind of food you feed your cat on. A vegetarian diet with proper nutrient profile is usually very effective in managing diabetes in cats.

Gastrointestinal Disorders - These disorders also include disorders of a cat's digestive system. These are disorders that hinder smooth digestion and absorption of nutrients contained in the food that your cat eats. Gastrointestinal disorders in particular interfere with both the intestine and stomach causing pain and in some cases swelling. Some of these disorders include acute gastroenteritis, colitis, diarrhoea, constipation, irritable bowel syndrome and pancreatitis among others.

Occurrence of these disorders presents several symptoms including vomiting, flatulence, body weakness, constipation, diarrhoea and in some cases regurgitation.

Although they do not present any immediate danger, gastrointestinal and digestive disorders can become life threatening if not addressed in good time. You need to take your cat to a vet for correct diagnosis and treatment. Treatment options available do aim at alleviating the pain and suffering that your cat experiences in addition to eliminating symptoms. One of the most effective treatment options available relates to the food that you feed your cat on. Vets do recommend highly digestible foods for cats with these conditions. Other recommended food types include high soluble foods.

You will be obligated to prevent occurrence of these disorders for the benefit of your cat. This will mean ascertaining specific factors or food that may be the cause of such disorders.

Heart Disease - Your Tonkinese cat is at risk of suffering from heart disease and like with most cat diseases, the food you feed your cat on plays a major role in preventing or encouraging the disease. There are however other factors that may cause heart disease in your cat including old age and heartworm among other factors.

Heart disease has the negative effect of enlarging your cat's heart, making it inefficient. In effect, the heart holds more fluid than it is supposed to hold. A clever way to go about preventing excessive fluid in your cat's heart is to feed it cat food low on sodium.

Heart disease presents several symptoms, some similar to those presented by other cat diseases. These include low-pitched cough, difficulty in breathing, weight gain/loss and abdominal swelling among other symptoms.

Urinary Tract Infections - UTIs are various infections that do affect both the bladder and urethra. Of the infections, feline idiopathic cystitis (FIC) is the most prevalent. Thought to be caused by excessive levels of stress, it causes inflammation of the urinary tract in addition to forming crystals along a cat's urinary tract. Such crystals are in most cases those of calcium oxalate.

UTIs present different symptoms including inappropriate urination, straining during urination, loss of bladder control, coloured urine, licking of the genitals, loss of appetite and lack of interest in any activity among other symptoms.

UTIs can be caused by several factors including obesity, diet composed of foods rich in magnesium, calcium, phosphorous and protein (unbalanced), surgery and infections. Any UTI can be very problematic since the reoccurrence rate remains high after treatment. This becomes real when a causative factor is not addressed before treatment is offered. Vets emphasize on the need to feed your cat on the right cat food that is not only nutritious but also well balanced.

Obesity - Acquisition of food in the wild for any creature including cats is not an easy task. Cats in the wild have to literally hunt and chase after their prey to feed on. The physical exertion definitely takes a toll on their bodies and it is therefore not easy to find an obese cat in the wild. Things are however different for domesticated cats including Tonkinese cats. Domesticated cats have it very easy when it comes to food simply because all that they eat is readily provided, which poses the risk of obesity.

From study findings of a research study conducted by the Association for Pet Obesity Prevention (APOP) in 2011, over 50% of cats in the USA were found to be either obese or overweight. It therefore simply means that your Tonkinese cat is also at risk of becoming obese even though it is one of the most active cat breeds you can find.

Simply put, your cat is most likely to become obese when its energy intake is more that the amount of energy it requires. Just like in humans, its body converts the extra energy it consumes into fat, which gets deposited in specific locations within its body. Getting rid of deposited fat can be a big challenge even with regulation of energy intake.

Living with an obese Tonkinese cat or any obese cat for that matter can be very expensive. This is so because obesity forms the foundation of a wide range of diseases and health conditions that will see you in and out of a vet's clinic on a regular basis. Just like in humans, obesity in cats causes such diseases as arthritis, heart disease, diabetes, cancer of the bladder and breathing difficulty.

The ideal weight of your Tonkinese cat should be between 15-26 pounds (7-12kg) and between 11-19 pounds (5-9 kg) for a male and female respectively. You need to take anything beyond these as a cause of concern. It is therefore important that you have your cat weighed whenever you call at the vet for regular checkups, which should ideally include weight measurement.

You should however be able to tell whether your cat is becoming obese or not even without weighing it. You should be able to feel your cat's backbone and ribs whenever you place your hand on its back. Failure to feel the bones should be a clear sign of obesity.

Obesity is a serious health condition in cats. Just like in humans, obesity in cats encourages occurrence of such serious diseases/health conditions as diabetes, heart disease and cardiovascular diseases. Ensuring that your Tonkinese cat maintains normal body weight goes a long way in preventing regular trips to a vet's clinic, which translates to reduced health care costs.

Your cat can become obese for several reasons, one of which is free feeding. Most cats left free to choose when to eat often develop obesity. This is so because a free feeding program gives a cat the opportunity to overeat, in effect consuming too much food that its body does not really need. Veterinarians recommend feeding your adult cat between two to three meals in a day with the amount of each meal controlled to avoid overeating. Ideally, your cat's food should be about half of a human meal.

The other main cause of obesity in cats is intake of too much calories. Unlike humans, your cat does not have the Amylase enzyme that digests carbohydrates contained in their food. The enzyme plays the very important role of breaking down large carbohydrate molecules into smaller absorbable units of glucose.

Furthermore, cats are not carbohydrate consumers by nature. Because most dry cat foods contain high levels of carbohydrates, you need to shop carefully for the same. Any dry cat food you buy should have minimal carbohydrates if any. It is highly recommended that you feed your cat a diet that is similar to its natural food, which makes canned cat food better. A cat's ideal diet should be high on meat-based protein and moderate fat and water.

Apart from carbohydrates and a free feeding program, the other main cause of obesity in cats is cat treats. Availability of cat treats has made many cat owners lazy when it comes to feeding their cats. Many cat owners rely on cat treats as their cats' main food. Cat treats contain high levels of carbohydrates and feeding your cat on them on a regular basis puts it at great risk of becoming obese. You should only feed your cat on treats at special occasions as a way of appreciation or reward.

Unlike in humans, obesity in cats is a non-hereditary health condition. Your cat will only develop obesity because of what you feed it on. It is therefore very necessary that you pay attention to what your cat eats and in what amounts.

Apart from food, you seriously need to ensure that your cat is physically engaged on a daily basis. Exercises are very important not only for your cat's physique but also in stimulating its mind. You need to make effective use of cat toys to help your cat burn excess fat deposits in the body.

Formulating a balanced and nutritious weight loss diet should also be effective in helping your cat cut down on excess body weight just in case it has already become obese. You need to formulate a diet that is low on carbohydrates but high on meat-based protein and other nutrients including fresh drinking water.

Pustule - Pustule in cats is what acne is to humans. Just like in humans who suffer from acne mostly on the facial area, your cat is also likely to suffer from acne that affects its chin although its lower lip can also be affected. Major causes of pustule in cats happen to be poor grooming (lack of it) and excess oil on the skin surface, oil produced from within the body.

Just like acne in humans, your cat is most likely to present such symptoms as black/whiteheads, swollen chin and development of nodules that can be very painful. Your cat can end up having boils as a result of pustule.

A vet will normally try to rule out such health issues as feline leprosy, allergy and skin tumour before diagnosing pustule. Confirmation of correct diagnosis is usually through such procedures as fungal culture, biopsy test and skin scrapping among other procedures.

For treatment, a vet will normally prescribe antibiotics, topical creams and shampoos. Regular occurrence of pustules should be a cause for concern regarding your cat's general health. It may be necessary for a vet to undertake your cat's full health scan to ascertain the exact cause.

Hypoadrenocorticism - This is what is commonly referred to as Addison's disease even in humans. This disease is mostly caused by an imbalance in the levels of both glucocorticoid (cortisol) and mineralocorticoids (aldosterone,) hormones produced in the adrenal gland. These two hormones play the very important role of maintaining your cat's good health and excess or insufficient production of the same leads to serious health complications. Excess or insufficient production of the two hormones impairs the function of the kidney, gastrointestinal system, the nervous system and the cardiovascular system.

Your cat will present a number of symptoms, which may include signs of depression, vomiting, bloody faeces, unexplained weight loss, general body weakness and lack of appetite among other symptoms. Apart from excess or insufficient production of the two hormones, the disease can also be caused by metastatic tumours.

A vet will normally perform elaborate laboratory tests, blood count and urinalysis tests in diagnosing if your cat suffers from Addison's disease. If so, he/she may recommend that your cat remains hospitalized for intensive therapy since Addison's disease is usually an emergency case. The first line of treatment is usually giving of body fluids intravenously with the aim of balancing the two hormones. Your cat will henceforth need to receive hormonal treatment throughout its life even with recovery.

Feline Asthma/Bronchitis - This is the inflammation of a cat's bronchi and bronchioles, which leads to the narrowing of the airways. Left untreated, asthma/bronchitis presents the risk of a cat developing excess tissue within its lungs, tissues that make it very difficult for the lungs to inflate.

In both acute and chronic asthma/bronchitis cases, a cat is most likely to present such symptoms as coughing, general body weakness, lack of appetite, breathing difficulties and skin coloration among other symptoms.

Although the exact cause of asthma/bronchitis in cats is yet to be known, your cat is most likely to suffer the same in case you smoke in the house, in which case your cat inhales the resultant smoke. The disease has also been linked to parasitic lung infection and in particular infection by lungworm, use of air fresheners at home and indoor chemical sprays.

Diagnosis of asthma/bronchitis in cats is usually through blood tests that also show whether it is acute or chronic. A vet may also need your cat's faecal sample to ascertain the presence of parasites. There are instances when a vet may order for X-ray imaging with the aim of ascertaining both the nature and extent of the disease.

Asthma/bronchitis in cats is usually a serious disease and your cat will most likely be given Oxygen therapy in addition to anti-inflammatory medications to reduce the swelling of the airways. A vet may recommend that your cat remains hospitalized for further investigation and monitoring.

Tyzzer Disease - This is a disease that mostly affects both kittens and young cats. It is a serious, life threatening disease caused by Clostridium piliformis bacterium that multiplies within the intestines before entering a cat's liver, leading to serious damage of the liver.

If infected, your cat will show a number of symptoms including general body weakness, signs of depression, loss of appetite, diarrhoea, low body temperature and abdominal distension among other symptoms.

Veterinarians diagnose Tyzzer disease through laboratory tests of blood, urinalysis and blood count among other diagnosis procedures. Diagnosis of the disease is usually revealed when there is a high level of liver enzymes. There is no treatment for Tyzzer disease and affected cats do die.

Capillariasis - This is a cat disease caused by Capillaria plica and Capillaria feliscati, parasitic worms. Although the parasites mostly affect a cat's urinary bladder, it can also affect its urinary tract. Your cat will most likely show signs of frequent urination that can be painful, bloody urine and straining when urinating.

Diagnosis of this disease is through urinalysis, which should reveal presence of Capillaria ova. A vet may offer injection or other forms of medications for treatment. The possibility of the disease recurring usually remains high especially if your cat is fond of venturing outdoors often. This is because it is outdoors where it has access to earthworms.

Hepatic Lipidosis - This is a disease of the liver that is commonly referred to as fatty liver. It is one of the most fatal diseases that affect domestic cats across the world. The liver plays the important roles of synthesizing proteins, producing digestive enzymes and detoxifying the body.

By its nature, a cat's liver cannot convert large amounts of fat into energy the way it is in humans. Failure by a cat's liver to convert large amounts of fat efficiently leads to accumulation of fat, which impairs the liver's function. Furthermore, the liver releases the accumulated fat that by then has turned yellow into the bloodstream, leading to yellowish eyes. Left untreated, a cat develops several health complications before dying of the disease.

Fatty liver can be caused by various health conditions and diseases including cancer, diabetes, kidney disease, inflammation of the pancreas and obesity among others. If affected, your cat will most likely present such symptoms as yellowish eyes, unexplained rapid weight loss, signs of depression, jaundice, vomiting, constipation and drooling of saliva.

A vet will normally perform routine laboratory tests of blood count, urinalysis and biochemistry profile in diagnosing the disease. Such other imaging tools as radiography may also be performed to examine the abdomen. You cat will most likely be hospitalized for treatment, which includes fluid therapy and vitamin B supplementation. A vet will obviously recommend an appropriate diet for your cat so as to prevent re-occurrence of the disease.

Sporotrichosis - This is a disease caused by the Sporothrix Schenckii fungus found in mould and yeast. Your cat can easily contract the fungus when it rubs against a surface with mould or yeast, in which case the fungus attaches to its skin before penetrating into the body. Your cat can also contract the disease when it inhales fumes from moulds.

If infected, your cat will most likely present such symptoms as skin lesions, swollen lymph glands and wounds on the head among other symptoms. This is a zoonotic disease that can be transmitted from human to animals and vice versa. It is therefore very important that you be careful when outdoors with your cat. In particular, your cat should not venture into areas with decaying organic matter.

In addition to physical examination, a vet will normally carry out laboratory fluid tests to diagnose the disease. Your cat will most likely be hospitalized for treatment that includes administration of anti-fungal medications.

Polyphagia - Polyphagia simply refers to a cat's increased appetite for food. It is a health condition where your cat simply starts demanding more food to the extent of becoming ravenous all the time. This condition can be caused by many factors and it is only appropriate that you ascertain the exact cause. Although your cat may gain weight, weight loss will be a sign that it is not well health wise.

In addition to increased appetite, your cat will most likely develop obesity or lose weight. Causes include onset of aging process, use of certain cat medications, diabetes and poor absorption of food.

Polyphagia is normally diagnosed through blood, urine tests and radiography imaging. Treatment normally takes into account the causative factor, which in case of a disease requires a vet to advise on the best management regime while treating the initial disease (causative factor).

Panosteitis - Panosteitis refers to the inflammation of bones in cats. It is a very painful health condition that affects the long bones found in a cat's legs. If affected, your cat will most likely limp before becoming lame. Although this condition mostly affects large-sized cats including Tonkinese cats, it can also affect medium-sized cats. It is, however, a treatable health condition that a cat can recover from to lead a perfectly normal life.

In addition to limping, your cat is also most likely to show such other symptoms such as signs of depression, fever, anorexia and weight loss among other symptoms. While the actual cause of this health condition remains unknown, diagnosis is through X-ray imaging and blood tests. Treatment of this health condition is usually limited to pain management in which case a vet is bound to prescribe anti-inflammatory and steroid medications.

Coprophagia - This is a health condition that normally worries cat owners. Your cat may suddenly start eating its own faeces after defecating. Although the actual cause of this condition is unknown, it is thought to be as a result of both mineral and vitamin deficiency in a cat's diet.

Apart from eating its faeces, you may also observe your cat eating rocks, clay and soap among other non-edible items. Your cat will also have diarrhoea and vomit frequently.

Apart from mineral and vitamin deficiency, other factors believed to cause the condition include malnutrition and such other diseases as thyroid disease, diabetes and increased appetite among other factors.

Diagnosing this health condition can be very involving. A vet will normally set out to ascertain whether the condition is a simple behavioral problem or a medical condition, in which case he/she will undertake a complete biochemistry profile, blood count and urinalysis. Treating this condition depends on the causative factor. While the change of your cat's environment may help in case the causative factor is ascertained to behavioral, a vet may prescribe specific medications should the causative factor be medically related.

Urine Incontinence - This is a case of lack of control of the bladder, just in the same way it is in humans. Your cat will present different symptoms in case it has this health condition. Such include frequent urination, wet hair between its rear legs or on the abdomen, skin inflammation around its genitals and wet bedding among other symptoms.

There are simply many factors that can make your cat lose control of its bladder. Some of these include neutering/spaying procedures that disrupt the nerves around the bladder, lesions on the brain, overactive bladder syndrome, UTIs, lesions on the spinal cord and underdevelopment of the bladder among many other causes.

Diagnosing urine incontinence in cats can be very challenging because of the many possible causes. A vet will however strive to ascertain the particular cause before designing an effective treatment plan that may take some time. Treatment normally depends on the ascertained cause.

Mesothelioma - Mesothelioma refers to a rare type of tumour that develops on the cellular tissue lining the interior part of a cat's body, the epithelial linings. These linings play the important role of protecting the internal organs by covering them. They also facilitate movement within the body.

Just like with other types of tumour, Mesothelioma develops when mesothelial cells fail to divide or replicate in the normal way before migrating to other parts of the body, which further spreads the tumour.

Your cat will show several symptoms if affected including difficulty in breathing, muffled lung/heart sounds, general body weakness, vomiting, inability to exercise and enlarged abdomen among other symptoms.

Diagnosing this condition normally involves a vet undertaking a complete blood profile, blood count and urinalysis. A vet may also obtain X-ray images of your cat's abdomen/chest, radiography and ultrasound to observe presence of masses in the body cavities. Drainage of unnecessary fluids within the body is usually the first line of treatment before medications are prescribed.

Stertor/Stridor - While Stertor refers to a cat's low-pitched, noisy breathing, Stridor refers to the high-pitched noisy breathing that your Tonkinese cat can exhibit. Stertor is most likely to occur when your cat inhales air. It is similar to snoring except that your cat's inhalation of air will be constricted, resulting in a low-pitched breathing occasioned by vibration of tissues that align the throat. On the other hand, Stridor is likely to occur when your cat inhales air with throat tissues in a rigid state.

Your cat will exhibit a number of symptoms when affected. These include inability to meow and extra-ordinary nature of breathing among other symptoms. These two related conditions can be caused by narrowed nostrils, inverted laryngeal, paralysis of the voice box/windpipe, tumour of the voice box and presence of foreign matter within the windpipe.

There are also risk factors associated with the occurrence of the two health conditions. Some of these include an environment with high temperatures, high metabolic rate, over-exercising and poor drinking/eating habits among other possible risk factors.

Diagnosis of the two conditions usually involves a vet obtaining your cat's health history, performing an internal imaging procedure (fluoroscopy) and X-ray imaging of the neck to identify any abnormalities in the neck's soft tissues. There are instances where a vet may need to perform surgery when foreign matter is lodged within the windpipe.

Baylisascarisis - This is what is referred to as Raccoon disease in cats. The disease also affects humans. It is transmitted by larvae of Baylisascarisis procyyonis parasite (roundworm) found in faeces left open in the environment. Your cat is most likely to contract the larvae in case it is used to venturing outdoors into areas with other cats having the parasite.

Your cat will present several symptoms if affected. These include un-coordinated walking, difficulty in swallowing, regular seizures and general confusion among other symptoms.

Diagnosis of this disease is through laboratory examination of a faecal smear test that should detect presence of the disease in your cat's intestines. The larvae should be seen through ophthalmoscopic examination. There are a good number of medications that a vet can prescribe for your cat including Corticosteroids and albendazole medications.

Abscess - Abscess refers to skin irritation. Just like in humans, cats also suffer from skin irritation. Although simple skin irritation can be treated using topical creams and ointments, serious cases of irritation can worsen especially when bacteria invades the affected area.

Skin irritation can be caused by a number of factors including fights with other cats, fights from which infected cats infect your cat with Pasteurella multocida bacteria, which causes skin irritation. Left untreated, the bacterium finds its way deep into the skin, causing other internal problems.

In treating skin irritation, a vet will normally recommend the use of topical skin creams/ointments as the first line of treatment. This can be in addition to antibiotics. A vet may undertake clindamycin treatment in case of serious skin irritation where the bacterium has penetrated the skin.

Hematuria - This refers to a condition where your cat's urine contains blood. This can be a serious disease since it may be a sign of a serious underlying process. One of the serious underlying diseases that cause hematuria is cancer. In most cases, female cats stand a high risk of suffering from hematuria compared to male cats.

Apart from cancer, there are many other factors that can cause hematuria. These include a low level of platelets in the blood, UTS's, kidney disease, anatomic disease and other metabolic diseases among other causes.

Vets do treat hematuria as emergency cases. It is therefore very important that you take your cat to a vet the first instance you notice your cat passing urine containing blood.

Idiopathic Epilepsy - This is a seizure in cats. It is a disorder that occurs in a cat's brain and causes sudden and in almost all cases uncontrolled/recurring attacks. If affected, your cat may or may not lose consciousness. Your cat will normally have a short aura and look as if it is under threat. It will eventually fall on its side at the onset of an attack and may salivate, defecate or urinate. An attack can last between 20 and 90 seconds before it recovers.

Seizures can occur when your cat is awake or when it is a sleep. The period soon after an attack is usually followed by such behaviour as general confusion, blindness, increased thirst, increased appetite and aimless wondering among other abnormal behaviour.

The exact cause(s) of idiopathic epilepsy remain largely unknown although it has been proved to be a hereditary health condition. Diagnosis of the condition normally involves blood cell count, thyroid screening and testing for viral infections if any. Treatment of this condition normally involves administration of anticonvulsant medications.

Constipation/Obstipation - Constipation is a condition where your cat finds it hard to defecate. The condition is characterized by incomplete, infrequent and defecation difficulty. On the other hand, Obstipation refers to worsened constipation. It is pronounced constipation characterized by lack of bowel movement, in which case a cat does not defecate at all.

You can easily tell when your cat has constipation. Apart from straining when defecating, it will also loose appetite. You may also notice swelling around the anus. Your cat is also most likely to produce hard and dry faeces with very little amount of urine.

Constipation can be caused by various factors including swallowed hair, swallowed bones, excess fibre in your cat's food, lack of exercise and low blood calcium among many other factors. It is very important that you do not allow constipation to develop further into Obstipation. It may be necessary to take your cat to a vet who will be able to undertake proper diagnosis of cause.

Treating constipation depends on the cause. A vet may recommend dietary supplementation or rehydration. A vet may also undertake manual removal of faeces in case of Obstipation. Surgery may be the only option in case of serious Obstipation. It is very important that you regularly monitor your cat's stool with the aim of detecting constipation in good time.

Hematoma/Seroma - Hematoma refers to a condition where blood collects in one spot outside blood vessels. On the other hand, Seroma refers to the same except that the collected blood does not contain any red blood cells; it is purely serum. Both hematoma and Seroma can occur in any part of your cat's body including within the ears and brain. The most common happen to be sub-dermal hematoma/Seroma that develops just under the cat's skin.

The symptoms that hematoma/Seroma present depend on the area of the body affected. Symptoms for sub-dermal hematoma/Seroma include swelling under the skin and itchiness around the area.

Hematoma/Seroma that develops in the head or brain presents such symptoms as seizures and coma. Hematoma/Seroma can be caused by various factors including trauma and in some cases serious insect bites.

It is very important that you give your cat a thorough physical examination when bathing. Doing so makes it possible to detect any unusual symptoms that may be of sub-dermal hematoma. A vet should be able to carry out physical and other tests on blood/serum drawn from the affected part for proper diagnosis. A vet can also perform imaging tests including X-ray, ultrasound, CT and MRI to diagnose internal hematoma/Seroma.

While minor hematoma/seroma do re-absorb and resolve on their own without any medication, a vet is obligated to undertake treatment procedures to resolve serious cases. Treatment involves draining the collected blood/serum and surgery in case of internal hematoma/Seroma.

Accidents - Although all cats are susceptible to accidents, Tonkinese cats happen to be at great risk of getting involved in accidents because of their playful nature. It is therefore very important that you make your home as cat friendly as possible by removing any sharp objects on the floor that they can fall on.

Serious injuries require that you take your cat to a vet at the earliest possible time since it can be life threatening.

Signs of Illness

Diseases do not develop overnight. It takes time before your cat finally falls ill. You need to be able to notice when your cat starts to show abnormal behaviour even before it falls ill. You can only do this having interacted and socialized with your cat to a point where you can easily tell when it is about to fall ill. Signs of illness in cats can be categorized into two; behavioural and physical signs.

Behavioural Signs

You should be able to notice different, unusual behavior by your cat, behavior that should prompt you to take your cat to a vet at the earliest possible opportunity unless you know the reason for any unusual behavior.

Although your cat will avoid its litter box when the box is unclean, avoidance of the same is usually a clear sign of a medical condition. Urination outside the litter box can be a sign of such medical conditions as diabetes, urinary tract infection or kidney failure. You need to take your cat to a vet in case you notice this unusual behaviour more than once when the litter box is perfectly clean.

Cats generally are not fond of drinking water. They obtain the water they need from their food. Although your cat will occasionally drink water, increased intake of water should be a cause for concern. This will be a sign of thirst, which is usually a sign of such health conditions/diseases as diabetes and hyperthyroidism among other diseases.

Failure by your cat to eat as it normally does should be a serious cause of concern. This may be an indication of loss of appetite, which may in turn be a sign of many diseases including gingivitis, trauma or anaemia among many other diseases.

Interacting and socializing with your cat should make it possible for you to know when and why it meows. Excess meowing (vocalization) may be a sign of stress, fear, sickness, pain or other medical conditions.

Your cat is most likely to spend a better part of the day and in particular during the morning hours sleeping. Although this is perfectly normal, excessive sleep in addition to hiding when it is awake should be a sign of fear, anxiety or sickness.

Being people-oriented, your Tonkinese cat will most likely get into the habit of welcoming you whenever you arrive at home. You will need to be concerned with any change in this habit. You will need to establish where your cat goes when not welcoming you. It is most likely that you will find your cat in its litter box, which should alert you of a medical problem.

Physical Signs

Unlike behavioural signs of sickness, physical signs are easy to notice and one of the most obvious signs you should be able to notice is a change in your cat's coat appearance. The fact that cats generally groom themselves means that your cat's coat should always be smooth. You should be concerned when the coat appears ruffled, which may be a sign of malnutrition, parasitic infection or such other skin disorders as ringworm or allergy.

Your cat should always have good breath. Bad breath will definitely not be normal since such may be a sign of diabetes, gingivitis, kidney disease or gastrointestinal disorder among other diseases/health conditions.

Any rapid weight loss or gain should be a serious concern. This is so because such may be a sign of many health conditions including malnutrition, overfeeding, diabetes, kidney failure or heart disease among many others.

Regardless of your Tonkinese cat's age, five very important factors determine how healthy it will be; proper nutrition and weight management, environment, good dental care, parasite control and vaccinations. The food that you feed your cat on determines whether or not it will remain healthy throughout its lifetime. You also need to make your cat's environment as friendly as possible to allow it to enjoy its life to the fullest. Ensure that you do not only socialize with your cat but engage in play activities as well.

Ensuring that your cat's oral health is at its optimum will also go a long way in preventing many diseases. Closely related to environment is the issue of parasites. Note that parasites thrive in unhygienic locations and it is therefore very necessary to ensure that your cat's room or space remains clean all the time. Lastly, you need to ensure that your cat receives all the recommended vaccinations and any other vaccination that may be fronted by relevant authorities from time to time.

When to Visit a Vet

When to take your cat to a vet depends on its age. Although kittens are in most cases sold off when they have already received the most important vaccinations, you will need to take yours to a vet at least three times in a year for any additional vaccinations or routine checkups. Doing so will make it possible for you to know any health issues that your kitten may have once it comes of age.

An adult Tonkinese cat does not require too much vet attention so long as you feed it on recommended foods and keep its environment clean. Your adult cat will have received the recommended vaccinations and should be in a position to remain healthy for a long time. You will however need to take it to a vet at least twice in a year for routine checkups.

Having an old or aging cat can be a bit of a problem because of the many visits you may need to make to a vet clinic. This is because it is during old age that such age-related diseases/health conditions as arthritis and heart disease among others set in. You will need to take your aging cat to a vet at least three times a year for routine medical checkups and for such indicated diseases/health conditions.

Your cat's general health remains squarely in your hands. You should take every step possible to ensure that your cat is not at risk of contracting any disease. You should be in a position to perform at-home physical examinations on a regular basis with the aim of determining your cat's general health condition.

Although you need to take your kitten, cat or aging cat to a vet as indicated, there are instances when it becomes necessary to take it to a vet at the earliest opportunity possible. Such incidents as accidents require that you take your cat to a vet for immediate medical attention.

The Veterinarian

The professionals commonly referred to as veterinarians or vets in short are actually veterinary physicians trained to treat diseases, disorders and injuries that affect non-human animals. Vets are referred to differently in different countries around the world. Although they are generally referred to as vets, they are professionally referred to as veterinary surgeons in the UK for instance.

Different countries have strict legislations when it comes to veterinary services, just the same way it is with human physicians. It is mandatory in almost all countries for anyone using the term vet to have undertaken the necessary training, registered and licensed to practice as a vet. Vets work in many institutions. There are those who work in vet clinics where they engage with animal owners or pet owners directly in treating their livestock. There are also those who work in such institutions as zoos, research institutions and animal hospitals.

Just in the same way that human doctors specialize in a specific area, vets also specialize. You are therefore most likely to come across a vet who is a surgery or dermatology specialist or one specializing in internal medicine. Generally however, vets diagnose and treat non-human diseases and health conditions in addition to providing aftercare and administration of vaccines. It is common practice to find vets in different countries working in the private sector. Only a small number work in government institutions. The fact that the majority work in the private sectors and in particular in clinics allows them to work directly with animal owners, owners whose animals have varied diseases and health conditions.

The fact that you plan to buy or already own a cat and a Tonkinese cat for that matter will obviously make it necessary to pay a vet a visit. This can be on the first day when you bring the cat home for the requisite vaccine(s). Just like with choosing your personal physician, you need to carefully choose a vet to engage for your cat's treatment and administration of vaccines.

How to Find a Good Vet

The fact that most vets work in clinics and private clinics makes finding the best vet a big challenge. This can be very true in case you live in a location where there are many practicing vets. The first way to finding the right vet is to enquire from close family members, neighbours and friends with pets. They should be able to refer you to a vet they personally know and who provides quality service.

Apart from making enquiries, you also have the option of consulting your local professional organization for information on licensed vets practicing in your locality. You also have the option of getting information on the right vets from a local cat breeder. A breeder in particular will be better placed to refer you to the right vet because he/she obviously engages the service of a vet to treat his/her cats in the cattery.

Whether you choose to make enquiries or contact a professional organization or a cat breeder, there are certainly several issues you will need to ascertain before you engage the service of a vet and one of these issues is whether or not the vet is licensed and enjoys some accreditation. A professional and ethical vet will normally share with you his/her certification, which should ideally be posted on the office wall. You will also need to ascertain whether or not the vet is a member of a local professional organization.

Apart from a vet's certification, accreditation and level of experience, you need to undertake an overall assessment of the facility with knowledge that it is at that clinic where you will henceforth be bringing your Tonkinese cat in case of health problems. It is therefore important to assess a facility's level of cleanliness among other issues.

It is common for vets to enter into agreements with pet owners for the purpose of taking care of their pets' health. Although most pet owners are in favour of such agreements as one way of cutting down on their pets' health care costs, doing so can be costly without due diligence.

It is possible that you and your pet's vet can have disagreements that force you to engage the service of a different vet. Terminating an agreement can be very costly depending on the agreement period you agreed upon. The best way to cutting down on your cat's health care costs is to shop for a suitable pet insurance policy that covers risks that your cat is susceptible to.

Cat Insurance

Your Tonkinese cat is not only people-friendly; it turns out to be the best companion you can have at home as a pet. Furthermore, it makes you active because of its playful nature. It is definitely a valuable family member. Just in the same way that you ensure your other family members are comfortable and in good health, you need to ensure that your cat also remains in good health and one way to go about this is to take out cat insurance for your Tonkinese.

It is a fact that veterinary fees and medication costs are always on the rise, which can make it impossible for you to meet your cat's medical costs at a time it needs it the most. Taking out an appropriate cat insurance policy goes a long way in keeping your veterinary costs low while giving your cat good health care.

Regardless of your location, any cat insurance policy you are likely to find is designed to cover the cost of veterinary fees and treatment of diseases/health conditions and injuries. Although very important, choosing the right cat insurance policy for your cat can be a big challenge. This is because there are simply many policies out there on the market that differ in terms of what they cover and price. This makes it necessary to know the best time to take out cat insurance.

The best time to take out cat insurance is when your cat is a kitten. This is because age is one of the most important factors pet insurance companies take into consideration when determining the level of insurance premium to quote. Kittens generally attract low premium rates compared to adult and aging cats that attract high premium rates because of various factors including onset of age-related diseases/health conditions.

There are generally four types of cat insurance policies you can choose from; lifetime, maximum benefit, limited time and accident-only policies.

Lifetime cat insurance policy covers vet fees for one year. You will need to continuously renew the policy to enjoy the same cover at the same premium rate regardless of how many claims you make. Although the cost of this policy is usually on the higher side, it is beneficial taking into account the fact that your cat remains covered for its lifetime even when it develops a life-long disease.

Unlike the lifetime policy, the maximum benefit policy provides cover for a pre-determined maximum amount of veterinary fees per health condition. The specific health condition is considered a pre-existing condition and is therefore excluded from future claims once the maximum limit is reached.

The time limited policy is similar to the maximum benefit policy except that the latter is limited to one year only, a period in which vet fees can be offset for each health condition.

The accident-only policy is limited to treatment of injuries your cat may sustain from accidents at home or outside the home including on the road.

A common feature of almost all cat insurance policies is the exclusion of pre-existing medical conditions. Such other procedures as preventative treatments, pregnancy/birth, neutering/spaying and worm control are also excluded from the policies. It is very important that you undertake some little research with the aim of finding a pet insurance company that quotes low premium rates on policies that provide a specific cover you need for your Tonkinese cat.

Chapter 11 – Cat Zoonotic Diseases

What is a Zoonotic Disease?

It is not enough to simply know diseases and health conditions your Tonkinese cat is susceptible to. It is also very beneficial for you to know the kind of diseases that you can easily contract from your cat. It is important to know that there are feline infectious diseases that affect cats only. There are also feline diseases that affect humans only. However, there are some infectious diseases referred to as zoonotic diseases that cut across, meaning that you can contract them from your Tonkinese cat and your Tonkinese cat can contract them from you. Simply put, zoonotic diseases are transmitted between humans and cats.

It is also important to note that although it is possible to contract a zoonotic disease from your Tonkinese cat, it is to a less degree than contracting a disease from a fellow human. Even so, it is extremely important that you take precautions, use common sense and maintain high hygiene levels particularly when handling your cat's litter box in order to prevent contracting any zoonotic disease that your Tonkinese cat may be suffering from.

Transmission of Zoonotic Diseases

Transmission of zoonotic diseases is mainly through direct contact. Simply put, you can easily contract a zoonotic disease from your Tonkinese cat when you come into contact with either your cat's excretions or secretions (saliva and /or faeces) in case it is infected. Similarly, you can also contract a zoonotic disease from your cat when you come into contact with food or water contaminated by your sick cat. Zoonotic diseases can also be transmitted by fleas and ticks referred to as vectors.

Risk

Although zoonotic diseases are not all that serious, there are categories of humans who are at great risk of suffering from them. Infants, HIV/AIDS-infected persons, elderly persons and patients receiving cancer treatment stand a higher risk of contracting and suffering from zoonotic diseases.

Common Zoonotic Diseases

There are five categories of common zoonotic diseases that you need to be aware of in order to protect yourself against them. They include:

Bacterial Infections

Of all zoonotic bacterial infections, bartonellosis (cat-scratch disease) is probably the most common. For instance, the disease affects about 25,000 people annually in the USA alone. You can easily contract the disease when your cat scratches or bites you in case it is infected. Apart from scratching and biting, bartonellosis can also be transmitted by fleas. You are most likely to present several symptoms of the diseases when infected. Such include swollen lymph nodes around your neck, upper limbs and head. Other likely symptoms include headache, fever, painful joints, general body weakness and lack of appetite. Although you can recover from the disease without any form of treatment, recovery can be after a very long time during which you suffer a great deal. However, the disease can be fatal to people with weak body immunity.

It is not mandatory that your Tonkinese cat presents symptoms when infected by the disease. It can actually look very healthy without showing any slightest signs of sickness. It is because of this that you not only need to trim your cat's nails but train it in such a way that it does not engage in biting or scratching humans and children in particular. In addition, you also need to control flea infestation.

The other common bacterial infection your Tonkinese cat can suffer from is Salmonellosis. This is a disease that causes serious fever, diarrhoea and stomach pain during the first days of infection. It is a disease that resolves itself without any treatment. Because of the serious symptoms that the disease presents, it may be necessary to seek medical treatment. This is because there is always the likelihood of the disease affecting your internal body organs.

Although you can also contract Salmonellosis by eating contaminated food such as chicken, you can also contract the same from a cat that otherwise looks very healthy (a carrier). Such a cat will pass salmonella bacteria in its stool. It is important to point out that the risk of your cat carrying the bacteria is high considering that it feeds on raw meat. You can however take necessary measures to protect yourself and your cat from contracting the disease by keeping your cat indoors and feeding it on raw meat bought or obtained from reputable outlets. You can also protect yourself from contracting the disease by wearing gloves when handling your cat's litter box and washing your hands thereafter.

Parasitic Infections
Parasitic infections are the other common zoonotic infections you can contract from your Tonkinese cat. Disease-causing parasites are in most cases transmitted externally by fleas. Although fleas rarely thrive on humans, they can bite and cause inflammation and itching of your skin. Letting your cat have fleas can also be dangerous considering the fact that flea-infected cats do end up having tapeworms as a result of ingesting fleas when grooming.

Apart from external parasites, you can also contract internal parasites from your cat. Such include hookworms and roundworms. Children are in particular at great risk of contracting these worms because they are most likely to touch contaminated soil and put their fingers in their mouth. It is therefore very important that you maintain a high level of hygiene and everyone in your home should thoroughly wash his/her hands before eating anything. In addition to buying anti-parasitic medications to prevent environmental contamination, you also need to take your cat to a vet for faecal examination for determination of presence or lack of internal parasites.

Fungal Infections

Fungal infections are the other category of zoonotic diseases that can be transmitted from humans to cats and vice versa. One of the most common fungal diseases is Ringworm. Contrary to common belief, Ringworm is not caused by a specific worm but by a group of fungi that causes infection that appears on the skin. If affected, your cat will present such symptoms as grey, dry and scaly patches on its skin. Most affected cats do happen to be those housed in overcrowded rooms. In case you are also affected, you are likely to present such symptoms as red, rounded and itchy lesions on your skin. Edges of the lesions will normally appear scaly.

Transmission of Ringworm is largely through contact with your cat's skin directly or through contaminated environment. Transmission of fungal infections can be very fast considering that fungal spores on your cat's skin will continuously drop off and cause infections. Because of the continuous dropping off of spores, eradicating the group of fungus from your house can be very difficult unless you take your cat for proper treatment. In order to prevent environmental contamination, it is very important to ensure that your cat remains free of fungus in addition to maintaining good hygiene.

Protozoal Infections

Protozoa happen to be organisms with a single cell. Such organisms that affect both cats and humans include giardiasis, toxoplasmosis and cryptosporidiosis. Both cryptosporidiosis and giardiasis are known to cause serious diarrhoea. Either you or your cat can easily contract the two protozoa from contaminated water but not from each other. You can easily prevent the two protozoa by taking your cat to a vet at least once a year for faecal examination, wearing gloves whenever you handle your cat's litter and litter box, washing your hands thoroughly after handling litter and draining off any stagnant water among other causes.

On the other hand, toxoplasmosis is caused by toxolasma gondii, a protozoon that causes serious illness. Although it is less likely to contract the protozoa from your cat directly, you can contract it from coming into contact with contaminated soil or water. Note also that you can contract the protozoa through eating undercooked food and in particular undercooked meat or vegetables. Those with a weak body immune system, children and pregnant women are usually at great risk of contracting the protozoa from the environment.

Your Tonkinese cat can contract the protozoon through eating rodents and/or birds that carry the protozoon. In case of infection, your cat will pass on the protozoon into the environment through faeces. The protozoon is very hardy since it can remain in the soil for many months from where it can contaminate gardens and water.

There are several ways through which you can prevent toxoplasmosis. One of these is by maintaining high hygiene levels, wearing gloves when handling your cat's litter box and when gardening. In addition, you need to ensure that all food is properly cooked.

Viral Infections
Viral infections are the last category of zoonotic diseases that you need to protect both yourself and your cat from. Although it is true that viruses only infect their host, human viruses only affect humans and feline viruses only affect cats, there is a deadly virus that can be transmitted between cats and humans; the rabies virus. You can easily contract the rabies virus from your cat in case it is affected when it bites you. In the case of your cat, the virus

attacks its central nervous system, leading to a wide range of symptoms.

Rabies infection is usually an emergency. This is simply because it is fatal. Although your Tonkinese cat is an indoor pet, you seriously need to ensure that it receives vaccination against rabies. In addition, you need to keep your cat away from coming into contact with wildlife and stray cats.

Protection against Zoonotic Diseases

Keeping a pet or pets and in this case a Tonkinese cat can be very fulfilling. It turns out to be not just a pet but also a valuable companion. You however need to be aware of the above-indicated common zoonotic diseases for your personal safety and that of your cat. It is therefore mandatory that you take the following measures:

- Maintain a general cleanliness of inside your house and outside as well.

- Always wash your hands after handling your cat and its litter box.

- Always wear protective clothing such as gloves when handling your cat's litter box.

- Do ensure that you take your cat to a vet for vaccinations and general check-ups that should reveal the presence of any zoonotic diseases.

- Do ensure that you maintain proper control of ticks and fleas.

- Prevent your cat from licking utensils and parts of your body.

- Feed your cat on quality and well-prepared cat food.

Chapter 12 – Vaccinations

What is a Vaccine?

A vaccine is basically a solution containing antigens that to the body's immune system looks like a disease-causing organism but is not. Your cat can be given a vaccine orally or through injection. When introduced into the body, the vaccine stimulates the body's complex immune system, making the system strong enough to fight any disease-causing organism that enters the body. Having your cat vaccinated is therefore very important.

Different jurisdictions have different vaccine requirements for all pets including cats. While some vaccines are only available in particular regions of the world because of prevalence of specific cat diseases, others are only available in other regions. There are basically two types of vaccines; core and non-core vaccines. While core vaccines are mandatory to all cats regardless of region or location, non-core vaccines are only found in specific regions or locations.

Like with anything introduced into the body, vaccines present several symptoms including fever, vomiting, loss of appetite, sluggishness, diarrhoea and swelling around injection area. There are also serious symptoms that may occur depending on the kind of vaccine your cat receives. These include life threatening allergic reactions and development of tumors around the injected area. The serious symptoms are however limited in occurrence. Vaccine symptoms are generally mild and do fade away within a few days.

Safety of Vaccines

Although cat vaccines are generally safe, there has been controversy around some vaccines that are often considered unnecessary. You need to appreciate the fact that it is because of feline vaccines that cats can now live beyond their expected life span. Production and administration of most vaccines that had raised controversies have luckily ceased. It is therefore perfectly safe to take your Tonkinese cat to a vet to receive the core vaccines. In any case, you are most likely to buy a Tonkinese kitten that is already vaccinated.

One major challenge that many cat owners face is when to have their cats vaccinated. There are different circumstances and instances when your Tonkinese cat needs to be vaccinated.

Kitten Vaccination

Your Tonkinese kitten or cat is most likely to have received its first vaccination while still with the breeder you bought it from. Even so, the vaccination must have been several weeks after it was born. This is because kittens naturally acquire sufficient immunity from their mothers through milk. Furthermore, a kitten's immune system is still not yet fully developed to receive artificial vaccination.

Breeders do arrange with veterinarians for their kittens to be vaccinated once they attain the age of seven weeks with additional vaccinations administered when they are twelve and again once they attain the age of sixteen years. The two additional vaccinations are in most cases boosters that fortify the first vaccination.

Adult Cat Immunization

Adult cats are not vaccinated but rather immunized. Like with vaccination, immunization is aimed at further boosting your cat's immune system to continue being effective in offering protection against possible infections.

Core Cat Vaccines

Core cat vaccines are those that all cats should receive regardless of location. These vaccines are very effective in offering protection against life threatening diseases found in all regions of the world. They include:

Feline Viral Rhinotracheitis (FVR) Vaccine
The FVR Vaccine is administered to protect against the FVR virus that is at times referred to as feline influenza or feline pneumonia. This is a respiratory disease found across the globe.

FVR is a highly contagious disease that can kill kittens within a few days of infection. The disease is easily transmitted through direct contact. One cat passes the disease on to another cat through saliva, nasal and eye secretions. When infected, your cat will most likely show such signs as coughing, sneezing, excessive nasal discharge, loss of appetite and high fever.

Feline Calicivirus (FCV) Vaccine
Your cat receives this vaccination to protect itself against the virus that causes respiratory infection. Occurrence of this disease usually ends in epidemic in areas with a large cat population because of its highly contagious nature.

FCV presents such symptoms as nose/eye discharge, mouth ulceration, anorexia and general body weakness at the initial stage. If affected, your cat is most likely to present such secondary symptoms as jaundice, high fever, swelling of the face and limbs (oedema) and dysfunction of organs within the body.

Feline Panleukopenia Virus (FPV) Vaccine
The FPV vaccine is one of the most important cat vaccines that your cat must receive. This is because the vaccine offers protection against the highly contagious and fatal diseases caused by the Panleukopenia virus that causes low white blood cells. The disease is largely transmitted through contact with bodily fluids of an infected cat.

If infected, your cat is most likely to show signs of severe dehydration, bloody diarrhoea, anaemia, depression, vomiting, loss of appetite, self-biting and loss of skin elasticity among other signs. Pregnant cats affected by the disease do give birth to kittens with cerebellar hypopasia.

Feline Immunodeficiency Virus (FIV) Vaccine

FIV is often referred to as feline AIDS. This is so because it is in many ways similar to human immunodeficiency virus (HIV). There are different types of FIV that the FIV vaccine is designed to protect against. Like in humans, your cat is most likely to live with FIV in case of infection in which case it will now be a carrier of the virus.

FIV attacks the immune system just in the same way that HIV does in humans. Although FIV and HIV are similar, humans cannot contract FIV and cats cannot contract HIV. Should your cat be infected, it will henceforth transmit the virus to other cats through saliva. Outdoor cats happen to be more at risk of contracting FIV virus compared to indoor cats.

Non-Core Cat Vaccines

Although classified as non-core cat vaccines, vaccines in this category are core in some regions of the world. This is because they are designed to offer cats protection against specific diseases only found in such regions. They include:

Feline Leukaemia Virus (FLV) Vaccine

FLV is a virus that causes life-threatening diseases in cats. One common disease associated with the virus is leukaemia, which develops when the virus destroys blood cells, in effect making them cancerous. The virus presents several symptoms including loss of appetite, poor coat condition, skin infections, fatigue, oral infections including gingivitis, diarrhoea and jaundice among many other symptoms. Your cat, if infected, will be able to transmit the virus to other cats through saliva, litter box (sharing) and food/water dishes.

Rabies Vaccine

Rabies was in the past a universal medical condition that affected humans, dogs and other warm-blooded animals such as cats. Vaccination campaigns undertaken in specific regions of the world made it possible for the disease to be eradicated in such regions. The rabies vaccine is now only common in specific regions where cats, dogs and humans are still vulnerable to Rabies infection.

Rabies is a serious disease that you should protect your Tonkinese cat from by ensuring that it receives the necessary vaccination. It is a viral disease that causes serious inflammation of the brain. It presents such symptoms as fever, loss of consciousness and restricted movement among other symptoms. Most rabies cases do result in death.

Chlamydophila Felis Vaccine

Chlamydophila felis is bacteria commonly found in cats. The vaccine for the bacteria is designed to protect against it. The bacteria cause inflammation of a cat's conjunctiva, rhinitis and respiratory health problems.

Depending on your location, you may be required from time to time to take your cat to a local vet for specific vaccinations aimed at preventing identified cat diseases in your specific area. Such vaccinations are in most cases occasioned by an outbreak of cat diseases. Different countries have legislations that make such vaccinations mandatory and failure to adhere to the same attracts different penalties.

Apart from being a requirement of legislation, you need to consider your cat's vaccination seriously. This is because you are the ultimate beneficiary knowing that your cat is fully vaccinated or immunized and therefore well protected from diseases that can affect its health. It is therefore very important that you consult your local vet on a regular basis for proper information on cat vaccinations and immunizations.

Chapter 13 – Costs

Estimated Monthly/Yearly Maintenance Costs

Owning a Tonkinese cat is very fulfilling. Not only is it a pet but a valuable companion as well. However, being responsible for your lovely Tonkinese comes at a cost, which you are obligated to bear. Although maintaining a cat can be very expensive, you can keep maintenance costs low so long as you stick to feeding it on an appropriate diet, ensuring that it receives all the necessary vaccinations/immunizations and maintaining proper hygiene at home.

You should be capable of maintaining your Tonkinese cat to make it different from any other Tonkinese cat or other cats on the street. Failure to meet some of your Tonkinese cat's needs and demands can easily be a cause of health problems. Furthermore, you stand the risk of losing your cat since it may simply run away onto the street.

There are different costs you are bound to incur when you plan to own and maintain a Tonkinese cat. You are most likely to incur heavy expenses when you prepare to buy or adopt one. Most of the costs relate to supplies that the cat will need soon after arriving at home. They include:

Food – There is no doubt that your cat will need to eat not just any food but quality cat food. This will be an incurring expense since you will need to buy quality food often. The cost of quality cat food averages at $120 - $150 (£71- £89) per month depending on your location. Yearly maintenance costs on food will therefore be around $1,800 (£ 1,072) in any given year.

Nutrition Supplements – These are dietary supplements that you may need to buy for your Tonkinese. You will however need to consult a vet before buying any. Ideally, it is a vet who should inform you when your cat needs supplements, which may be because of a special need. You may need to incur about $100 (£60) at any given time on dietary supplements.

Food/Water Bowls – These are supplies you will need to buy before you bring your kitten or cat home. Note that sharing of food/water bowls used by your cat will not be allowed. For instance, you should not feed your dog on the same food/water bowls used by your cat. Quality food/water bowls retail around $10 - $30 (£6 - £18) depending on your location. Note that you may need to replace the same at least twice in any given year, which makes yearly costs on food/water bowls between $60 - $90 (£35- £54).

Treats – Treats are edible foodstuffs that you will need to feed your cat on once in a while. They are actually niceties that you use as rewards when your cat does something positive. You are most likely to offer your cat treats more often during the first few months as you subject it to training, in which case you are bound to incur between $30 and $100 (£18 - £60) per month. Yearly treat costs average between $60 and $300 (£35- £178).

Grooming Supplies – Like with all cats, the Tonkinese cat is naturally a clean cat that goes the extra mile to keep itself as clean as possible. It will therefore groom itself often to achieve this. You will however still need to groom your cat, in which case you will be obligated to invest in quality grooming supplies. While you are bound to spend around $50 - $100 (£30 - £60) in buying permanent grooming supplies such as tools, you will spend between $30 - $60 (£18 - £35) on such other recurrent supplies as shampoos and odour removers every month. Your cat's yearly grooming costs will average between $200 and $500 (£120 - £300).

Cat Bed – Your Tonkinese cat will need a good place to sleep in and investing in a quality cat bed is highly recommended. A cat bed lasts a long time and you may only need to replace it when it is very necessary. A quality cat bed retails at between $20 and $100 (£12 - £60) depending on your location.

Cat Carrier – Like human babies, you will need to invest in a quality cat carrier for use in transporting your cat. Cats are generally not fond of travelling in cars and having a carrier makes travelling with your cat trouble-free. A quality cat carrier will set you financially back by between $20 and $100 (£12 - £60). You may only need to replace it after two or three years.

Cat Toys – Your cat is a playful and very active pet. This is why investing in quality cat toys is not only highly recommended but also very necessary. Having toys around will not only engage your cat in play but will also go a long way in helping it release a lot of energy it has, energy that if it would not use will make living with your cat a little bit of a problem. Quality cat toys retail at between $20 and $50 (£12 - £30) a piece and since you will need to buy different types, you should be ready to spend anything between $100 and $250 (£60 - £150) on toys once in a long time.

Clothing – Although a Tonkinese is a haired cat, it may be necessary to invest in cat clothing especially when you live in a region where it remains cold most of the time. Such is for use when it is extremely cold to a point where your Tonkinese cat shivers. There are indeed warm clothing specifically designed for kittens and cats that you need to consider investing in for your kitten's or cat's comfort. Such clothing cost around $100 and $250 (£60 and £150), depending on your location and clothing material.

Scratching Post – Having a cat at home presents the risk of having your furniture scratched. This is because cats have a natural scratching instinct. The best way of dealing with the risk of having your furniture scratched is providing your cat with a scratching post, which costs between $50 and $100 (£30 - £60 only once.

Proper care of your Tonkinese is not limited to making food and the other supplies available. You also need to ensure that your cat is in good health. Veterinary service will therefore be very necessary, at a cost. There are different veterinary services your cat requires. They include:

Routine vet exams – These are routine vet exams a vet undertakes with the aim of determining your cat's health condition. This can be three times in a year for a kitten, twice for an adult cat and thrice for an aging cat. You will be obligated to incur between $50 and $200 (£30 - £120) for such exams in any given year depending on your cat's age.

Vaccinations/Immunizations – Although you are most likely to adopt or buy a vaccinated kitten, there are immunizations it will need to receive once it comes of age. Such immunizations cost between $50 and $150 (£30 - £90) per year, depending on your location.

Spaying/Neutering – You may choose to have your cat spayed/neutered, in which case it will not be able to bring forth offspring. Having your cat spayed/neutered will cost you between $150 and $300 (£89 - £180), a one-off expense.

Emergency Care – You certainly will not rule out your cat getting injured, which will require emergency vet care. Depending on the nature of injury and your location, you are most likely to incur between $500 and $2,000 (£300 - £1,190) on emergency care, which may involve surgery.

Veterinary costs can be huge to the extent that they exceed any other cat maintenance expenses. This is why many cat owners choose to buy cat insurance policies that cover risks that their cats are exposed to, something that you too may consider.

Maintaining your cat requires that you be ready to commit yourself financially to its overall well being and health. On average, your Tonkinese cat's monthly maintenance cost will range between $400 and $700 (£238 - £416) monthly and therefore around $1,500 - $5,000 (£890- £2980 in a year.

Maintaining a cat can indeed be a very expensive undertaking. There are however several ways through which you can cut down on maintenance expenses and one of these is buying cat food in bulk. You can cut on cat food expenses by almost 50% by simply buying in bulk. The best way of realizing this is to buy at wholesale price, which guarantees you attractive discount.

Apart from cat food, cat treatment is the other recurrent expense you are most likely to incur throughout your cat's life. Taking your cat whenever it falls sick or when it gets injured and paying out of pocket can be very expensive. You need to consider taking out the best cat insurance for your cat. It will be appropriate to shop for a cat insurance policy that covers most of diseases and health conditions that your cat is susceptible to.

It is not mandatory to buy your cat's equipment including toys. You can effectively make use of locally available materials to make such equipment as scratch post, cat bed, cat tree and food/water dishes. You can make these as DIY projects or engage the service of a local artist to make them for you at a very minimal cost.

Chapter 14 – Care for an Aging Tonkinese Cat

Major milestones have been achieved in the last decade or so when it comes to treatment of cat diseases and management of cat health conditions. Improvements of existing cat medications and discovery of new cat treatment methods has made it possible for cats to live much longer than their expected lifespan.

Although all cats of all ages benefit from such improvements, aging cats happen to be the biggest beneficiaries. This is because properly cared for aging cats can now age gracefully without necessarily experiencing the pain and a lot of discomfort that aging cats hitherto experienced in the past.

Although your Tonkinese cat generally has a lifespan of between 15 and 18 years, it can live to attain the age of 20 years and slightly above so long as you provide it with proper care including veterinary care.

What is aging?

Aging is a process that every living being goes through. It is a natural process that sets in when life expectancy is attained, which in this case is 20 years for the Tonkinese cat breed. One day in a cat's life is a very long time taking into account the fact that a year in a cat's life is similar to about 15 years for humans. Likewise, a cat aged 15 years is like a human being aged 85 years. Just like in humans, the onset of aging in cats brings with it several challenges, some which can make your cat very uncomfortable if you do not offer the necessary help.

Physiological and Behavioural Changes

Your Tonkinese cat will exhibit many changes once it attains old age. One of the most visible changes is the tendency to walk on its hocks. This is because its hind leg muscles become weak to a point where running and jumping becomes difficult. This is the time to change its bed to a larger one because it finds it difficult to curl up in a small bed.

Your aging cat will also be very forgetful. It may choose to remain outdoors in case it ventures out regardless of the weather. This is also the time when it can easily get lost in case it is used to venturing out without company.

A visible sign of aging in cats is usually what is referred to as winding down. This is when it grows thinner with its hip, shoulder and backbones becoming visible. In addition to becoming thinner, the fat layer just under the skin also melts away, further exposing the bones. It is important at this stage to consult a vet for advice on special types of cat food and dietary supplements to feed your cat on.

The aging process also causes many faculty changes in a cat's life. Its hearing and cognition abilities diminish to a great extent. Furthermore, its metabolic rate also decreases. In case your Tonkinese is not used to venturing outdoors, it is bound to feel cold most of the time. It is your responsibility to ensure that your cat sleeps in warm beddings in addition to taking it out to receive sunshine when it is possible.

One fact you need to remain alert to when your cat ages is the fact that its immunity reduces, making it highly susceptible to many infections. It becomes very necessary to take your cat to a vet whenever you notice any strange behaviour or symptoms for immediate vet care.

Although Tonkinese cats are people-oriented pets, your aging Tonkinese cat will be more attention seeking than at any other time. This is because it naturally knows that it is incapacitated in many ways and will want to be near you most of the time for comfort, assurance and help. Your cat will however tend to sleep for a much longer time.

Because of the many behavioural and physiological changes that your cat is bound to go through once the aging process sets in, it is most likely to engage less in physical activities. It is however very important that you exercise your cat's mind. Limited physical exercise is also necessary to help your cat overcome any discomfort it may experience because of such diseases as arthritis, which aging cats are highly susceptible to.

Health Challenges in Old Cats

Your aging Tonkinese cat experiences a lot of changes including reduced immunity. This exposes it to many diseases/health conditions that you must take note of with the aim of helping it cope. Some of the health challenges your cat is most likely to face include:

Parasite Infestation

Your aging Tonkinese cat will probably not groom itself as it used to do. This exposes it to parasite infestation and in particular ticks and fleas. This will likely happen if it is used to going outdoors. Infestation of these parasites will easily lead to skin infections. The likelihood of your cat becoming anaemic also becomes high. This is when it becomes necessary to use flea spray or powder. Although you have the alternative of using flea collars, they have the disadvantage of being ineffective. Furthermore, flea collars can also cause allergic reaction.

Your cat is also likely to have internal parasites in case it is used to going outdoors, just in the same way it used to do when it was a kitten. It becomes necessary for your aging cat to receive treatment for worms and in particular roundworms after every three months.

Blindness
In addition to such health challenges as hearing loss and loss of memory, a major challenge that your aging Tonkinese is likely to face is blindness. This starts as partial loss of vision before developing into total blindness.

Although you may not be able to know when your cat is losing its vision, there are specific signs you need to look out for. These include reluctance to move, misjudging heights, clumsiness, eye rubbing, large pupils and when it easily gets startled. Because treating blindness due to old age is simply impossible, the best you can do to help your cat cope is ensure that it moves in a secure environment, offer help all the time and speaking to it often.

Pain
Such diseases/health conditions as arthritis that your aging Tonkinese is susceptible to are usually accompanied with pain. Your cat may tremble, shiver or crouch. It becomes very important to understand your cat's body language with the aim of offering help. It becomes necessary to take your cat to a vet for proper diagnosis of existing disease and for appropriate pain medications.

Dental Infections
Old cats are highly susceptible to dental infections. Indeed about 70% of all old cats suffer from dental infections mostly caused by the formation of plaque. It is during your cat's old age that you must ensure that it receives regular dental care that involves removal of plaque that forms tartar, which in effect leads to gingivitis.

Arthritis
Arthritis is the most common health problem that cats in old age suffer from, just like in humans. This health condition is usually accompanied by joint pain, pain that can make your cat very uncomfortable. Your cat will find it very difficult to engage in

physical activities. The best way to help your cat cope is to consult with a local vet for the best supplements to buy; supplements that support the rebuilding of joint cartilage.

Reduced Heart Function
Just like in humans, your cat's heart function reduces once old age sets in. Its heart muscles do not only weaken but also enlarge. It becomes necessary to take your cat to a vet for regular checkups and medications that strengthen heart muscles.

Chapter 15 – What to Do With an Old Tonkinese Cat

Living with an old cat or an old Tonkinese cat for that matter can be a serious challenge, especially if it becomes senile. You simply will not cope with the amount of care it needs to continue living comfortably. It is because of this that you may look for alternative ways on how your cat can still receive proper care until when it dies. You have three options:

Cat Rescue Center

Taking your aged Tonkinese cat to a dedicated cat rescue centre may be your only option of letting your aged cat go. Although it can be very difficult, doing so will lessen your burden of having to watch over it all the time.

Cat rescue centres are institutions established by such organizations as animal welfare societies. Such centres are usually staffed with qualified pet personnel with the necessary skills on taking care of pets of all ages. In addition to admitting aged pets including cats at a small fee, they also offer younger pets for adoption. Such do include rescued pets or those born in such institutions.

Most cat rescue centres are funded by donations received from pet lovers and other organizations. Some well established cat rescue centres serve as educational institutions where pet lovers have the opportunity to learn more about pets they are interested in buying or adopting.

Taking your old Tonkinese to a cat rescue centre does not in any way mean disposing it off. Most rescue centres allow owners to visit their aged cats, a good opportunity to reconnect with pets they have lived with for a long time.

Euthanasia

Euthanasia is the other route or option you have when it comes to dealing with your old cat. Most cat owners whose cats are aged choose to have their cats euthanized instead of taking them to cat rescue centres. The main reason for this is the fact that having their cats euthanized eliminates the worry they would otherwise continuously have over their pets at such centres.

Simply put, euthanasia is the practice where life is ended. You may choose to have your aged cat euthanized in order to relieve it from the pain, anguish, suffering and discomfort it goes through as it waits for its natural death. Different jurisdictions have different laws relating to euthanasia for humans and pets. Your vet should be in a good position to enlighten you on what laws apply in your jurisdiction.

Just like in the case of humans, a vet will normally require that you sign a consent form before euthanizing your cat. The signing of the form absolves a vet from any claim you make thereafter that he/she caused your cat's death. There are however certain instances where vets request pet owners for permission to euthanize their aged pets. Such cases are usually when vets discover serious diseases in the cause of treating cats. Even in such situations, cat owners have the last word on whether or not their cats should be euthanized.

Whether you take your cat to a vet clinic to be euthanized or call a vet to undertake the procedure at home, the procedure is the same. The procedure normally involves giving an over-dose of anaesthesia into the main vein in one of its forelegs. In case of difficult or troublesome cats, a crush cage is normally used.

Injection of anaesthesia leads to immediate unconsciousness followed by slow death. Your cat is most likely to exhale and pass urine as body muscles relax after death. To ensure that your cat is indeed dead, a vet may give additional injection of anaesthesia into the kidney or the heart. Your lovely cat will most likely die with eyes open and a vet will simply close the eyes before placing the cat in a position where it appears to be just asleep. It is only after this that a vet wraps your cat in a black bag both for safety and privacy before handing it over to you.

Watching your cat die can be a very traumatizing experience. The experience can remain in your mind for a very long time. This is why some cat owners choose to remain in a separate room when a vet undertakes euthanasia on their aged cats and other pets.

Most cat owners do choose to call a vet to perform the procedure in their homes rather than at a vet's clinic, a move that you too may consider. This is because having the procedure undertaken at home is somehow less traumatic.

The cost of euthanasia varies from one region to another and from one vet to another. The cost can actually be on the higher side if you choose to call a vet to undertake the procedure at home. Generally, the cost ranges between $30 and $80 (£17- £35) across the world. It is always recommended that you settle any outstanding amount with a vet before he/she undertakes the procedure. This is because you may not find it comfortable talking about payments when your cat is already dead.

Home Care
You may choose not to take your aged Tonkinese to a cat rescue centre or have it euthanized. You may take this route if you are fond of your cat and have the time to provide it with all the necessary care it needs until it dies natural death. Although most cat owners choose to care for their cats at home until they die, the suffering, pain and anguish they go through can similarly be traumatizing.

Taking your aged cat to a cat rescue centre may eliminate your responsibility to dispose of the body when it finally dies. This will depend on the agreement between you and a care centre management. Most centres do undertake to dispose of bodies of dead cats. Depending on your arrangement, you may be informed. Having your cat euthanized at a vet's clinic, at home or if you choose to care for your cat at home, you will have to determine how to dispose of the body.

Body Disposal

There are a number of ways through which you can dispose of your Tonkinese cat's body. Below are just some of the ways:

Burial

Burial of pets is fast becoming popular around the world and it is highly possible that you too may choose to bury your Tonkinese cat when it finally dies. Even so, you need to acquaint yourself with your local by-laws that relate to disposal of dead pet bodies. You will need to bury your cat soon enough before it putrefies unless you have a freezer where you can store the body for a few days. You may choose to bury your cat in your back garden or at your local authority's pet cemetery.

Even so, there are instances when you may not be allowed to bury your cat. Such are instances where the body poses a degree of risk to human health. This may apply if your cat dies of rabies in which case it will be the responsibility of a vet to dispose of the body.

Cremation

Like with burial, cremation is another popular way of disposing of dead bodies. You may choose to have your cat's body cremated to give you the opportunity to bring its ashes home in a jar to scatter in its room/space or simply keep. It is common to find pet cemeteries having pet cremation facilities where you can have your cat cremated.

Taxidermy

You may choose to have your Tonkinese cat taxidermized to at least allow you have it at home although in a static state. Taxidermy is a process where a professional taxidermist removes all the cat's internal organs including tissue and bones. The remaining skin is then stuffed to make your dead cat look real.

Desiccation

At times referred to as freeze-drying, desiccation is the process where water is removed from your cat's body. Your cat will simply be put in the right posture before being desiccated. The process can take as long as six months and most cat owners do like the result because of its lifelike nature. Because of environmental factors, the desiccated body is usually housed in a glass container for preservation. This gives you the opportunity to have your cat at home even though dead.

Resin Preservation

This is another way you may choose to dispose of your dead Tonkinese cat's body. It involves removal of blood and other body fluids, which are replaced with resin. Resin has the characteristic of setting in solid, which in effect yields a lifelike body.

Post-Disposal Period

The period soon after disposing of your cat's body can be a very trying time. It can indeed be a trying time in case you have another Tonkinese cat and other pets at home. Do cats have feelings? Will they realize that one of them is missing? How will they cope knowing that one of them is missing? It is a fact that cats have feelings. Tonkinese cats in particular develop a strong bond between them and will therefore be troubled with the absence of one of their own.

One thing you may notice when you have two Tonkinese cats as pets is that each of them marks its own territory. One of them naturally becomes the leader of the other. The absence of one of them therefore traumatizes the remaining one. It may take some time before the remaining one adjusts. The best way to comfort the remaining one is to always give it as much attention as possible.

The situation can be very complicated to handle in case you have children. This is because Tonkinese cats get along very well with children because of their playful nature. Your dead cat will not have just been your kids' companion but a valuable playmate. They are bound to take its death very hard. The best you can do in such a situation is to make your kids understand what death is and why their playmate has died.

Making your kids understand what death is and that it applies to human beings can be very beneficial to them. This is because kids learn through experiences and knowing about death will make them appreciate the fact that death is natural and can happen to any family member at any time.

How to Cope with Your Tonkinese Cat's Death
Your cat's death can be similar to the death of your child or a young family member. Knowing that you adopted or bought it, nurtured it to maturity and was a valuable companion that is no more can take a toll on your mind. Not only will you develop a feeling of loss but will grieve for your cat. You will probably go into a state of denial, develop anger and mourn before accepting that your lovely Tonkinese cat is no more. This may be the appropriate time to share your feelings with other family members. Doing so will no doubt go a long way in overcoming your anger and feelings of loss you may develop.

One reason why many cat owners choose to dispose of the bodies of their cats is to have the opportunity to remember their cats knowing that it is buried in their backyards. Remembrance provides you and your family with a good opportunity to reflect back on the good times you had with your dead cat.

Replacing Your Dead Tonkinese Cat

Having lived with a Tonkinese cat that is no more will most likely drive you to adopt or buy another to replace the dead one. When to have another one will however depend on several factors. One of the most important factors that may make it necessary to have another Tonkinese soon after the death of the previous one is if you had two of them.

The loneliness that the remaining one will feel may make it necessary to get another one for company. You may also need to have another one soon after in case you have children. The other reason why you may need to replace your dead cat soon relates to why you bought or adopted the dead one in the first place. You may simply like pets and Tonkinese cat in particular. You may also be used to having a pet as a companion and cannot do without one.

Chapter 16 – Becoming a Tonkinese Cat Breeder

The Tonkinese cat breed is gaining popularity with most cat lovers who are used to keeping hairy cats as pets. Indeed, demand for Tonkinese kittens and cats is on the rise. This is evident by the high prices quoted by Tonkinese cat breeders for purebred Tonkinese kittens/cats and by the rising number of breeders interested in the breed. You may choose to become a Tonkinese cat breeder to satisfy the rising demand or to promote and preserve this breed of cat.

Who is a Breeder?

Basically, a breeder is one who is engaged in the business of carefully mating selected animals or plants to reproduce offspring that exhibit specific qualities and characteristics unique to a breed. Becoming a Tonkinese cat breeder therefore involves breeding purebred Tonkinese cats with the aim of reproducing kittens that exhibit qualities and characteristics unique to the breed.

You can become a breeder purely for fun as a hobby, to promote the breed or as a business. Whether you choose to breed as a hobby or as a business, you will have a good opportunity to participate in professional cat shows and competitions. Becoming a breeder does not require that you must have attained a specific level of education. You must however demonstrate that you have compassion and a genuine interest in the Tonkinese cat breed.

Things to Note

Although you may have compassion and interest in the Tonkinese cat breed to a point where you want to become a breeder, there are important things you need to take note of. From the onset, becoming a Tonkinese cat breeder will not make you rich overnight. Becoming a breeder can be very expensive and you should not expect to recoup your expenses within a short period. You need to start breeding as a hobby before you can expect to start receiving some income. Indeed, most current successful Tonkinese cat breeders started off breeding as a hobby before graduating to full time commercial breeders.

The second thing to note is that the practice of breeding requires commitment, devotion and time. Time in particular is very important. It becomes very necessary that you devote most of your time to your cattery. This is because the cattery requires daily cleaning, feeding, grooming and treatment of your cats. This is the only way you will be able to breed healthy Tonkinese cats that will encourage many in your neighbourhood to buy.

Thirdly, becoming a breeder requires some level of financial investment. You will need to construct a cattery at a suitable location, install the necessary infrastructure, buy cat food and engage the service of a vet among other costs. You will also need to incur other expenses in having your cats registered by relevant bodies and pay some fee to your local authority. Most current Tonkinese cat breeders started off with only two cats in small rooms right within their homes, something that you too may consider.

Lastly, you need to be prepared to handle the emotional toll that comes along with the practice of breeding. The fact that you will be taking care of many cats and mating them means that they will be giving birth. It is common for some pregnant cats to die when giving birth in catteries. Others will die of natural causes including diseases. Kittens will also be at risk of dying of natural causes. Watching as your lovely Tonkinese cats and kittens die will take a serious toll on your mind.

Where to Start

The best way to start off as a breeder is to prepare a room in your home to serve as your cattery on a temporary basis. This is not only cost effective; it will also be easy to manage your cats. Such preparation involves equipping the room with all the necessary equipment and supplies your cats will need to survive. These include food, water/food dishes, a scratch post, bed and beddings and cat play toys among other equipment and supplies. You also need to engage the service of a veterinarian who will be responsible for treating your cats whenever they fall sick, get injured and in giving vaccinations.

The second step to becoming a Tonkinese cat breeder is identifying an established breeder to buy kittens or cats from. It is mandatory that you buy from an established and registered breeder. This is because such a breeder will be breeding pedigree Tonkinese cats that are properly registered.

You have the option of buying a female Tonkinese cat (queen), in which case you will be obligated to buy a male (tom) afterwards or take the queen to a vet or breeder for insemination. You also have the option of buying two Tonkinese cats; a tom and a queen. Depending on your preference and level of preparedness in becoming a breeder, you may choose to buy kittens or adult cats.

The fourth step to becoming a breeder is to register as a breeder. You have several options on how to register, depending on your location and preference. There are both national and international cat registries from which you can choose one to register with. International cat registries include UK's Cat Fanciers Association (CFA), France's Federation Internationale Feline (FIFe), UAE's Emirates Feline Federation (EFF), The American Cat Fanciers Association (ACFA) and The International Cat Association (TICA). National cat registries include UK's Governing Council of the Cat Fancy (GCCF), UK's Felis Britannica (member of FIFe), PRC's Cat Aficionado Association (CAA) and the Canadian Cat Association (CCA) among other national registries.

Registering your cats provides for several benefits. First, you will be recognized as a registered breeder licensed to breed Tonkinese cats. Secondly, you will have the opportunity to participate in both national and international cat shows and have your cats participate in different championships depending on their age. Participation in such championships can earn you good money depending on how your cats perform.

Thirdly, you will have the opportunity to learn better breeding techniques both from a registry you register with and other Tonkinese cat breeders. Registering as a breeder also gives you the opportunity to know the exact breed standards you will have to maintain as a Tonkinese cat breeder. Lastly, you will have the opportunity to be appointed as a Tonkinese cat show judge after gaining reasonable breeding experience and if you so wish. Note that you can register with more than one registry if you so wish so long as you are financially capable of meeting all registration fees.

Different cat registries do organize different Tonkinese cat shows and competitions. CFA for example organizes the Kitten Shows and Championships (for pedigreed kittens aged between one and three years), Championships (for unaltered cats aged eight months), Premiership (for altered cats aged above two year), Veteran (for both altered and unaltered cats aged seven years) and Household (for non-pedigreed cats aged two years months).

General Breeding Information

Successful registration as a Tonkinese cat breeder is just the first step to becoming a professional breeder. Because the cats you buy will have been registered by their breeder, you will need to register the litter that your cats give birth to. This you will do with a registry you registered with. Registering your litter entitles you to a unique prefix that will henceforth be used as the first name for all litter that your cats will produce. It will be your responsibility to indicate a prefix you will wish to use.

Different cat registries have different requirements when registering prefixes. The GCCF for example requires that you must have been registered as a breeder for at least one year before you can register your litter.

Unlike some cat breeds that take up to two years to become sexually active, Tonkinese become sexually mature reasonably fast. Both your tom and queen become sexually active with the queen capable of attaining pregnancy when it is between one and two years old. You will be able to know when your queen is on heat when it becomes too vocal and lies on the floor as if presenting itself to a male.

Your queen's gestation period is between 60 and 65 days. The last week of pregnancy will see your queen look for the most appropriate place to give birth. It will look for dark yet safe place where to give forth its litter. Tonkinese cats generally give birth to average litters, between two and five litters.

Building a Cattery

It is only appropriate that you build a cattery once you have established yourself as a Tonkinese cat breeder. A cattery is where you house your cats for commercial purpose. Although yours will be a breeding cattery, you will also have the option of using it as a boarding cattery in which case other cat owners not able to travel with their cats will bring their cats to you for safe keeping at a fee.

It is mandatory that you apply for a license from your local authority before you can build a cattery. You also need to follow cattery building guidelines provided by a registry you register with. Every registry has minimum cattery construction requirements that you must stick to before you can receive another license from the registrar. A registrar will only grant you a cattery license after inspecting your cattery and certifying it to have met the set minimum construction requirements. Most registrars engage the service of local veterinarians to undertake search inspections. It will be the responsibility of the appointed vet to inspect your cattery on a regular basis to ensure that you stick to set breeding guidelines.

There are several minimum requirements when it comes to constructing a cattery, one of which is space. Your cattery needs to be spacious enough to accommodate all your cats comfortably. The minimum space per cat is set at 30 cubic feet. In addition, you need to create a space for play, grooming and maintenance. Established breeders do go the extra mile to group and house their stock according to their age, groups that are housed in separated cages as one way of preventing diseases.

The other very important minimum requirement you need to meet is to construct your cattery in such a way that it allows for free flow of fresh air for your cats' good health. Your cattery should not only have enough windows but large enough windows that allow for free flow or air in and out of the cattery. The fact that Tonkinese cats are both indoor and outdoor pets makes it very necessary that you have windows that allow sufficient amount of light into the cattery. Artificial lighting may be necessary to achieve this if the windows do not provide for sufficient natural light.

Cat registrars are very strict when it comes to cattery sanitation. Not only are you required to construct your cattery in a clean environment; you will also need to ensure that there is high standard of cleanliness in and around your cattery on a daily basis. Sanitation is one of the most important things that an appointed veterinarian will always pay attention to whenever he/she pays a visit to your cattery.

Such guidelines are not only requirements, they are mandatory taking into account the fact that failure to observe the same can lead to occurrence of cat diseases that can wipe out your cat population. Apart from such guidelines, you will need to have all the necessary supplies and equipment that your cats will need for good health and play activities. You will also need to engage the service of a veterinarian who will be available whenever situation demand and when it is time for vaccinations.

Chapter 17 – Organizations, Associations and Clubs

There are many international and national organizations, associations and clubs that are in the business of promoting and maintaining the welfare of specific cat breeds, including the Tonkinese cat breed. Most of the international and national organizations and associations are indeed cat registries. Cat clubs in particular are of special mention because they limit themselves to specific cat breeds including the Tonkinese cat breed. Most clubs happen to be established by cat owners. Below are just a few of the notable organizations, associations and clubs.

Tonkinese Breed Association (TBA)
This is a group of Tonkinese fanciers in the USA. It is affiliated to CFA. The group does not impose any restrictions on membership and is open for anyone interested in the Tonkinese breed. However, majority of those admitted happen to be either Tonkinese cat breeders or exhibitors. Non-breeders and exhibitors can however join as associate members with no voting rights.

Based in the USA, the group was established to promote the breed by providing information about the breed to members of the public. The group is also very active when it comes to rescuing lost Tonkinese cats that are eventually taken to cat rescue centers.

The group performs a number of activities geared towards promoting the Tonkinese breed. Such activities include publication of an informative quarterly magazine (Aqua Eye) that is distributed to members and the general public and sponsoring of a Tonkinese cat show every year in each of USA regions on a round-robin basis.

Tonkinese Breed Club
The Tonkinese Breed Club is a dedicated club for Tonkinese cat fanciers in the UK. It was established in 1991 and although its membership is largely made up of Tonkinese cat breeders, it also accepts individual members with interest in the breed.

The club organizes a number of Tonkinese cat shows in different parts of UK. In addition, the club has most of the time ready Tonkinese kittens for sale.

Tonkinese Cat Club
Tonkinese cat Club was established in 1994. It is based in the UK and has been affiliated to GCCF since 1998. In addition, the club is also affiliated to Feline Advisory Bureau (FBA). Membership of the club includes Tonkinese cat breeders, exhibitors, owners and individuals with interest in the breed.

The club organizes a number of Tonkinese cat shows across the UK in collaboration with other cat clubs. In addition, the club is exists to promote the breed and rescue lost ones.

Tonks West
Tonks West is a Tonkinese cat club based in the USA. It is affiliated to CFA and caters for Tonkinese cat breeders, exhibitors and owners located in the western part of USA. It also draws its membership from Canada.

With the slogan "A Sea of Aqua", the club's offices are located in San Bernardino Fairgrounds in Victorville, California.

Canadian Cat Association (CCA)
CCA was established in 1961 by a small group of Canadians eager to have a national feline registry. All Canadian feline registrations were hitherto done in the USA and Europe. Indeed all cat shows in Canada were under the auspices of feline associations in the USA. It is currently the only national feline registry in Canada.

The establishment of CCA paved the way for the establishment of different feline clubs across Canada, clubs set up by cat owners and lovers of different cat breeds. The association is not only involved in registering and promoting different breeds of cats including the Tonkinese cat; it also organizes cat shows across Canada.

The American Cat Fanciers Association (ACFA)
Founded in 1955, ACFA serves the interest of cat breeders, cat owners, exhibitors and the general public in different ways. The association largely engages in promoting welfare, providing education, knowledge and enhancing interest of domesticated cats, both purebred and crossbreed.

Membership to ACFA is open to all including members of the public with interest in cats. Members receive several benefits including a copy of the association's regularly published ACFA bulletin that is published seven times in a year. Members also have access to many cat articles on the association's website, articles written by professional cat breeders and vets.

Membership to ACFA also entitles one to vote in the association's yearly elections. Members have the obligation to elect from among themselves who to represent them in the association's board of directors. ACFA is also a cat registry that you can register your litters with as a breeder at massive discount.

ACFA organizes cat shows at different locations in the USA, an activity that gives cat owners including Tonkinese cat owners an opportunity to showcase their pets and possibly win show awards.

The Cat Fanciers' Association (CFA)
Founded in 1906 in the USA, CFA is the world's largest cat registry of pedigree cats. Headquartered in Ohio, the association has a mission to preserve and promote pedigree breeds of cats with the aim of enhancing their well being. CFA current cat breed registration stands at 43 including the Tonkinese cat breed. CFA has witnessed unprecedented growth since 2006 after its

centennial celebrations, growth that has seen the association recognize 39 breeds for its Championship Class.

In addition to registering cat breeds, CFA also offers several other services to purebred cat owners, catteries and the general public. It indeed has registered cat pedigrees that date three generations back.

Perhaps one of the most memorable moments for CFA was in 1994 when it hosted the CFA International Cat Show, the largest in USA cat shows. In addition to organizing cat shows, CFA is also engaged in setting and enforcing cat breed standards through cattery inspections, training cat show judges, supporting and publicizing research on cat issues, influencing cat legislation agendas and running cat breed rescue programs.

Cat Owners Association of Western Australia (COAWA)
Founded in 1992 in Western Australia, COAWA exists as a cat registry and an advisory body to the Coordinating Cat Council of Australia. COAWA registers pedigree cats and provides a platform where cat breeders, cat owners and members of the public meet. It also registers non-pedigree cats.

In addition to cat breed registration, COAWA also organizes cat shows including kitten and adult championship shows. The association currently has four cat clubs affiliated to it and boasts of a good number of cat breed judges.

The Governing Council of the Cat Fancy (GCCF)
Founded in 1910, GCCF is the largest cat registry in the UK. It largely registers pedigree cats. GCCF was founded by smaller cat registries and is now an independent council with over 150 member clubs including Tonkinese cat clubs across the UK. In addition to being a cat registry, GCCF also licenses cat shows organized by all cat clubs affiliated to it. It currently licenses over 100 cat shows every year. Apart from licensing cat shows organized by its clubs, GCCF also organizes its own cat show

dubbed the Supreme Cat Show, which is usually the largest cat show in the world.

The International Cat Association (TICA)

TICA is the world's largest single cat association. Its membership comprises of catteries, cat owners and people interested in cats. Based in the USA, TICA draws its membership from across the globe including from Africa, Latin America, North America, Europe and Asia. It is a cat genetic registry that also registers new cat breeds. In addition to registering pedigree cat breeds, TICA also registers non-pedigree household cats that enjoy the same status as pedigree cats in terms of cat shows and awards.

In an effort to enhance cat breeding, TICA has an elaborate Junior Exhibition specially tailored for children who love cats, giving them a good opportunity to graduate to senior levels as cat breeders.

TICA has clear responsibilities that include registration of both pedigree and non-pedigree litters, formulation of regulations for management of cat associations, licensing of cat shows organized by its members, establishing cat breed standards, dissemination of cat breed information, organization of cat exhibitions and education of cat owners among other responsibilities.

World Pet Association (WPA)

WPA is a body that exists to bring pet food manufacturers and pet owners together. It allows for the two parties to interact through education and sharing of information. Most of its members happen to be cat food manufacturers, cat breeders, cat organizations and associations. WPA is basically the cat industry's premier trade association. It plays a very important role in disseminating information, educating and supporting research related to cat food.

World Cat Congress (WCC

WCC is a confederation of the largest international and national cat organizations and associations. It exists to promote understanding and cooperation among all the organizations and associations on matters that concern them. It encourages international cooperation among its membership on such matters as veterinary issues, legislations, pedigree issues and other related matters. Its membership includes FIFe, CFA, TICA, WCF, ACF, GCCF and NZCF among many other international and national organizations/associations.

Conclusion

Cats and Tonkinese cats in particular make very good pets. You will never feel bored when living with a Tonkinese cat. It is a playful cat that engages you all the time. It will always want you to give it attention, which is perfectly normal since it may be the only trusted companion you can have at home.

The Tonkinese cat is one cat that does not discriminate when it comes to family members. It is particularly very good with children to who it develops a very strong bond because of its playful nature. Furthermore, the cat is very receptive to training.

According to research studies published in the Journal of Vascular and Interventional Neurology, living with a cat provides for several health benefits. One of the main benefits is that living with a cat reduces the risk of suffering from cardiovascular diseases including heart attack. Other health benefits associated with living with a cat include reduced risk of high stress level, reduced cholesterol level and reduced risk of depression.

Children raised in an environment where there is a cat have also been noted to grow up healthier than those raised in an environment where there is none. Unlike most cat breeds, the Tonkinese breed is very cost effective so long as you give it proper care. It is generally a healthy breed that is less susceptible to common diseases that other cat breeds are highly susceptible to. The fact that the breed's kittens do not inherit serious diseases/health conditions translates into reduced veterinary expenses.

Conclusion

The popularity of the Tonkinese across the globe is not in doubt. It is one of the top cat breeds that most homeowners prefer to have in their homes as indoor and outdoor pets. Its popularity is also evident in the increasing number of cat breeders registering with different cat registries around the world. It is also not surprising that dedicated Tonkinese cat clubs are also being established in different regions around the world.

You can choose to have two Tonkinese cats as indoor pets or join the big league as a Tonkinese cat breeder. While you will a cat that is loyal, obedient and a valuable companion if you choose to have them as pets, you are also most likely to excel, as a breeder should you decide to go that route.

Published by IMB Publishing 2014